# RUN FOREVER

# RUN FOREVER

## YOUR COMPLETE GUIDE TO HEALTHY LIFETIME RUNNING

**AMBY BURFOOT**

First published in the USA in 2018 by
Center Street, part of Hachette Book Group

First published in Great Britain in 2018 by
ARENA SPORT
An imprint of Birlinn Limited
West Newington House
10 Newington Road
Edinburgh, EH9 1QS

www.arenasportbooks.co.uk



ISBN 978-1-909715-60-8
eBook ISBN 978-1-78885-091-9

Some names have been changed to protect the identities



*British Library Cataloguing-in-Publication Data*
A catalogue record for this book is available on request
from the British Library.

Designed and typeset by Polaris Publishing, Edinburgh

Printed and bound by MBM Print SCS Limited, East Kilbride

This book is dedicated to all my teachers and mentors, particularly John J. Kelley. And also to the many great athletes, coaches, and scientists who have shared their running knowledge with me through the last 50-plus years.

# CONTENTS

# INTRODUCTION

Running is the simplest of sports. It deserves a simple book. That's why I wrote *Run Forever*.

In the last twenty-five years, running has grown massively popular and increasingly complex. There are too many shoes, drinks, energy bars, training plans, stretching devices, massage tools, and books willing to dissect and discuss all of them.

I'm here to say the opposite: Running is not complicated. *Run Forever* doesn't attempt to explain everything there is to know about running. It only explains what you need to know. It drills down to the essentials.

I've organised *Run Forever* in a clear and easy-to-follow manner. There are just six main sections: Getting Started, Running Nutrition, Going Farther, Dealing with Injuries, Gaining Speed, and Running Forever. Even though it contains a Half-Marathon Training Plan and a Marathon Training Plan, which some might consider the ultimate running challenges, Going Farther precedes Gaining Speed. Both require consistency and determination. But Gaining Speed is the harder of the two, because it also demands specialized workouts and true grit.

Each section has an additional ten to twelve 'chaplets', as I call them. These provide short, concise summaries of key information, and conclude with at least three direct actions to follow.

Everything you'll read on these pages has emerged from my half-century of running experience, the testimony of the world's best runners and coaches, and the scientific conclusions of top running researchers.

At the personal level, I've road tested every piece of advice in *Run Forever*. Over the last fifty-five years, I've run 110,000 miles – more than enough to make lots of mistakes (bad for me) and figure out a better way (good for you).

Once I was fast. I was fortunate enough to win the Boston Marathon in 1968, and to run a 2:14 that year. Now I'm slow. I'm a happy member of the 'back of the pack' gang. And I'm proud to be there.

I've finished the same Thanksgiving Day 5-miler fifty-five years in a row. A few days after this book is due to be published, I hope to complete the Boston Marathon on the fiftieth anniversary of my win in 1968. Along the way, I've run marathons with Will Ferrell and Oprah Winfrey. If they can do it – and both did, finishing their races impressively – so can you.

Many friends helped me write this book. In four decades of work at *Runner's World* magazine, I had long discussions with hundreds of elite runners: Frank Shorter, Bill Rodgers, Kathrine Switzer, Grete Waitz, Joan Benoit Samuelson, Deena Kastor, Meb Keflezighi, Ryan Hall, Shalane Flanagan, and more. Their wisdom and insight is woven throughout *Run Forever*.

I also have a consuming interest in sports science, and have interviewed many of the leading lights of the last half-century – Ken Cooper, David Costill, Ralph Paffenbarger, James Fries, Jack Daniels, Tim Noakes, Steven Blair, and more. Their evidence-based findings underlie the most important concepts in *Run Forever*.

My high-school coach and mentor John J. Kelley, winner of the 1957 Boston Marathon, played a bigger role than all others combined. Not because he compiled a lengthy list of running rules, but because he lived true. He taught me that one's actions, philosophy, and guiding principles – the simple, big-picture stuff – are far more important than the day-to-day minutiae. I try to remember this lesson every day, and to live by it.

Certain themes return frequently in *Run Forever*. That's because they are so central to healthy running. One of these is a practice I call 'adaptive excellence'.

I believe we should always aim high, but appropriately. Today it takes me two hours longer to finish the Boston Marathon than it once did. But I'm still moving along. To every thing, there is a season – a time to run fast, and a time to run slow and relaxed. But we must continue to pursue excellence, even as we adapt to new circumstances.

Other themes: Listen to your body. Less is sometimes more. Hills are good for you. Recovery is a necessary part of peak performance. Run-walk builds fitness many different ways. Patience and consistency are eternal virtues.

In my twenty years as executive editor of *Runner's World* magazine, we regularly asked readers how long they planned to continue running. The response was always the same: Ninety-nine percent said they wanted to run for the rest of their life.

That's my goal too. And I bet it's also yours. Ultimately, it's the main subject of *Run Forever.*

Running doesn't get easier with age, but the payoffs grow greater. While none of us can be guaranteed that running will add years to our life, there's no doubt it will add life to our years. Which is far more rewarding.

The most important contribution of *Run Forever* is its emphasis on the mind. The book begins with a Brain Training chaplet, and ends with one. That's because I believe running is not so much a physical challenge as a cognitive one. Running doesn't depend on the size of your heart, the length of your legs, or the cholesterol content of your blood. They are entirely secondary. Your brain rules all.

You don't need to do twenty-five squats today to build your quad muscles. You need to think five positive thoughts about your motivations for running, fitness, and lifelong health. Because it's not the quads that will get your legs moving, it's the thoughts.

Life is not a part-time sport. It's a full-time challenge. President Roosevelt said: 'The credit belongs to the man who is actually in the arena, whose face is marred by dust and sweat and blood; who strives valiantly.' Few would disagree with this view.

No one wins every race, but we are the better for engaging. If we sit on the sidelines, we can only wither away.

I believe that every run is a new adventure, and every mile a gift. I hope *Run Forever* will make you feel the same.

Stay the course. Run long and healthy.

AMBY BURFOOT

# SECTION 1

# GETTING STARTED

# My First (Horrid) Run

MY FIRST LONG-distance run was one of my worst. Maybe *the* worst ever. It came as a form of punishment. Too many runners get their start this way. It's all wrong. Indeed, it's no doubt the main reason so many stop running – an initial, painful introduction to the sport.

I hope you'll find a different way. In fact, it's essential. If you don't organise your running as a positive part of your days and weeks, you won't continue it for long. I was lucky, as you'll learn in a moment. You might not be so fortunate. In that case, you'll need to discover ways to create your own luck – to surround your running with many positive reinforcements.

I grew up the son of a YMCA director. He introduced me to all the popular sports – primarily American football, basketball, and baseball – and I played them all with a wide-eyed energy and enthusiasm. I like to think I was pretty good, too. I grew nearly a foot in junior high school, reaching the six foot mark.

That helped me choose my first high school sport. I decided to take a shot at basketball. It seemed a good fit. I had a burning desire to be a star athlete. I would do whatever it took.

I tried out for the basketball team in the winter of my first year in high school, where I was a tenth grader. More scrappy than talented, I somehow managed to survive the cut, and was placed on the J.V. squad. At the very bottom of the squad. I was the worst player on the team. Even I could see that. Before this, in my inexperienced youth, I hadn't realised how many basketball players were stronger than me, not to mention better jumpers, better dribblers, better shooters . . . the whole works.

The coach saw fit to put me in only one game. As I recall, we were behind by about thirty-seven points with 2 minutes remaining. Coach figured it was safe to let me play at that point – nothing to lose. Not for the team, not for his personal reputation. Both were already scraping the bottom of the barrel. His assessment proved accurate. In my 2 minutes of play, I performed no miracles.

That first season of J.V. basketball shocked me to my senses. I realised I hadn't reached the brink of athletic stardom, but didn't know where to turn next. At one practice, coach grew particularly exasperated by our efforts. He threw up his hands in despair, and ordered us off the court. As punishment, he told us to run the school's 3-mile cross-country course. 'You guys aren't tough enough,' he said. 'Maybe cross-country can teach you a lesson or two.'

None of us were excited by the prospect, but what were we to do? I was the quiet, obedient type, so I set off at a dutiful pace behind my peers, the better basketball players. To my surprise, most of them were walking after a quarter of a mile. I kept going.

It turned out that, while I was the worst player on the basketball team, I was better than the others at running 3 miles. I'm not saying I enjoyed the run. Hardly. It was absolute torture, especially the two big hills on our high school's cross-country course. I struggled to keep running on the hills. My teammates walked.

If our basketball coach intended to punish us with this workout, he succeeded. By the end, my face was caulked with salt, and my thighs felt as heavy as a tree trunk. Worst of all, my feet were raw and blistered. To wear high-top basketball shoes on a cross-country run is a little like using a wooden matchstick to brush your teeth. You can get the job done, but you know that better equipment would make things much more pleasant.

At any rate, I finished minutes before anyone else. And soon found myself calculating my sports skills: Did I want to be last in basketball, or take a chance at a new sport where I seemed to have some natural talent?

I chose the latter. It made all the difference.

I had never met my cross-country coach John J. Kelley until the first day of practice the following September. Still, everyone in my high school knew about Kelley. He was a Boston Marathon winner (1957), two-time US Olympic marathoner, and still among the half-dozen best marathoners in the country.

I soon learned that these were the least of Kelley's accomplishments. More important, he was a brilliant, iconoclastic, unique individual – way ahead of his time. Kelley was a vegetarian, organic gardener, Bob Dylan fan, peacenik, ardent environmentalist, raconteur, student of great literature and philosophy, and a believer in the essential goodness of all people, especially artists, free thinkers, and the downtrodden.

I understood little about running at the time, but of course it had a terrible reputation. Cross-country was for skinny, weak, uncoordinated kids who couldn't catch or throw. Worse, it was tough, sweaty, boring, bone-wearying, soul-sapping, and completely unrecognised by newspapers and the sports-loving public. My school's cheerleading squad didn't even show up at cross-country meets.

I didn't care. I only wanted to be good at something. I was even willing to endure the endless tedium of interval training on a track, if that's what it took. In the early 1960s when I joined Kelley's cross-country team, everyone did interval training. Almost every day.

Kelley wasn't 'everyone', however. He followed a different drummer. We never ran endless loops around the cinder track that circled the football field. Instead, he led us on romps through apple orchards, nearby parklands, and marshy trails at the edge of Long Island Sound.

Kelley never spoke a word about how to run. I have no list of ten commandments that he proffered us. There were no quizzes. He just showed us how he ran, and we followed along like he was the Pied Piper, amazed by the wonders of almost every workout. For more on Kelley running, see the essay introducing Section 3, Going Farther.

For Kelley, there was just running and being – living for the moment. We youngsters didn't realise that we would win state championships based on this training. We just had fun scrambling over walls, sweating up long hills, scampering along narrow, rocky paths, and exploring the world around us.

It is the way I have run ever since, and I highly recommend it to you. Gadgets and gizmos can be nice, but you don't need them. Running partners are fantastic, some of the time. Training plans can establish good guidelines, but be careful that you don't fall into the perfectionism trap. Don't let running rule your life; it doesn't have to.

Instead, use running to enhance your life. Think big. Run free.

# 1

# The Brain: Training Your Most Important Muscle

EVERY BEGINNING RUNNER I've known has had many mistaken notions about running. Some believe you must have long legs to be a good runner. Some believe a large heart is necessary. Others figure you need cavernous lungs to process vast quantities of oxygen.

Many are convinced you must be rail-thin. Or possess muscles that have been well developed by other sports like soccer or basketball. None of these are true.

Running is a non-skill activity. Think for a moment about tennis. If you don't learn the serve and backhand, you won't go far in the game. Think about golf and all the clubs toted around by pro golfers. Each club requires a different skill set. It takes years to master just a few of them.

Not so with running. There's nothing to learn. Unless you had a childhood disability, you mastered running when you were three years old. It was as easy as talking and walking. Today you can put one foot in front of the other as skilfully as an Olympic marathoner. You aren't as fit or as fast, but you don't lack any key techniques.

To improve your body's ability to run, only one organ is required – the one between your ears. You got it, the brain. If you can tap into the power of your brain, you will succeed. You will become a healthy, accomplished runner, capable of achieving any goals you aspire to.

Want to complete a marathon some day? No problem. Tens of millions of others have done this. They didn't have more talent than you. They simply set their minds to the task.

It's not about shoes, it's not about nutrition, and it's not about conquering the hills. Those will come. They are important. But they fade away to almost nothing when compared to the brain.

I'm not saying you'll have a tailwind at your back every step of the way. I don't believe in gauzy promises wrapped in pretty pink bows. That's not my style.

Quite the contrary, I can guarantee you'll face plenty of setbacks and disappointments in your running. Everyone does. But these obstacles won't stop you, not when you run with your brain.

**Don't be perfect. Be persistent:** Runners tend to succeed in all areas of life, not just in running, because they are organised, committed, consistent, disciplined, and goal-oriented. These are all brain functions. You need a plan, and you need to follow that plan. But you don't have to be perfect. You just have to be persistent.

If you can check off 80 percent of the workouts on your plan, that's roughly as good as 98 percent. So don't get discouraged when illness, bad weather, family emergencies, or a thousand other responsibilities blow up your best-laid plans.

Just get re-organised, re-dedicated, and back on track. Use your brain to chart a new course. It's your most potent weapon.

**Practise resilience:** Bend but don't break. When the going gets tough, you need to get tougher. Whenever you miss a short-term goal, visualise yourself hitting that goal just a little farther down the road. Nothing is impossible, but everything takes time – and often more time than we would like.

Running is a Tortoise and Hare activity. The Tortoise always gets to the finish line first. She doesn't set records. She just gets the job done. Winners never quit, and quitters never win.

**Dream big:** In his insightful book, *Why We Run*, zoologist and ultramarathon runner Bernd Heinrich, PhD, explains why humans run long distances, but other animals don't. It's because we have the largest brain. Palaeo man dreamed of catching an antelope, the yummiest and most nutritious meal imaginable.

He knew it might not happen in the first hour, but he didn't quit. He stayed on the trail. He kept on trekking. No other animal would do this, because none could look into the future and see their ultimate success. Humans could. It is how we humans have accomplished everything. We hunt our dreams.

Today a beginning runner can imagine completing a 5K race in three months, even if she can't finish a mile today. A runner can dream of weighing 180 pounds in a year, even if he weighs 250 today. A runner can dream of seeing her daughter graduate from college in fifteen years even if her oncologist has just delivered a grim report.

Dream on. When you harness the awesome power of your brain, your legs will follow.

# 2

# Minutes, Not Miles

TOO MANY RUNNERS are obsessed by miles. They measure everything in miles. How far they run in a day. In a week and a month. In a year and a lifetime.

Miles are okay. After all, our races are measured in miles (or kilometres). Our cars keep track of miles covered, our now-ubiquitous GPS systems know exactly how many miles it is from here to there.

But beginning runners should avoid running by the mile. It's much smarter to run by the minute. That's why the Walk-Run Programme coming up on page 19 doesn't tell you how many miles to run. It only tells you minutes.

Here's the problem with miles. If you measure a mile, you're also going to measure your speed. It's inevitable. We've all got clocks on our wrist or our smartphones, and we all live our lives according to what these clocks say.

As a result, any time you run a certain number of miles, you're going to divide the distance by the time it took you. That will give your pace or speed. The two represent different ways of expressing the same thing. Runners talk about their pace per mile. For example, someone might run a 10-minute mile (10:00 pace). That's the same as a speed of 6 miles per hour.

But speed is the wrong thing for beginning runners to measure. Speed leads to a dark and perilous place. It tempts you to run a little faster each day. You'll try to improve from 15 minutes per mile, to 14 minutes per mile, then to 13, and so on. This is a trap any runner can fall into, but it's particularly alluring and dangerous for beginning runners.

Dangerous? Yes. Here's why. Speed kills. Not literally, but it stops your fitness progression. There comes a time in a runner's life when it's completely normal, healthy, and motivating to pursue faster running. But that's not when you're a beginner. Speed kills beginners by increasing the risk of injury, burnout, failure, and discouragement.

So don't go there now. Don't run by the mile. Instead, run by the minute.

There's no pace in a minute. It's an empty canvas. No matter how you paint it, you can't go wrong. If you aim for 30 minutes, and complete 30 minutes, you have met your target. There's nothing else to measure yourself against. You can't fall short.

You get to 30 minutes, you have won. You are on your way.

**Remember Kipling:** We have no reason to believe that Rudyard Kipling was a runner, but he certainly thought like one. Especially when he wrote:

*If you can fill the unforgiving minute*
*With sixty seconds' worth of distance run,*
*Yours is the Earth and everything that's in it.*

Smart, that Kipling. He knew the minute was the true measure of human endeavour, not any particular distance, be it a kilometre or mile. Follow his advice. Don't fret over miles. Content yourself to fill the minutes of every run, and to reap the rewards.

**Keep a log:** It's important to keep track of your running days and minutes. Runners do this by establishing a training log of some kind. I've heard arguments that the best, most motivating log is a simple sheet of paper on the refrigerator. Makes sense. You can hardly ignore a refrigerator log, and it might serve a nutritional purpose beyond its primary role.

Of course, there are many other ways to record your running these days, including your computer's hard drive, fitness trackers, smartphone apps, and watches, and dozens of websites. It doesn't matter which you choose. But keeping a log keeps you honest and provides a record of your journey. So do it.

Aim for pleasure, not for pain: When you run for time rather than speed, you can fill your mind with more than just 'Push, push, push'. That's the beauty of running by the minute. Think about pleasure, not pain.

Admire the sounds and sights of nature, feel the warm glow filling your body, or check out the small changes in your neighbourhood. Let your mind wander. I've always been amazed by the random and intriguing thoughts the pop up out of nowhere when I'm running. I won't claim they're genius. But they keep me amused. I've never been bored.

Running gives you a special time to get better acquainted with yourself. I find that a wonderful bonus.

# 3

# The Wisdom of Slow

OLYMPIC MARATHON CHAMPIONS do 80 percent of their training at a slow, comfortable pace. As a beginner, you should do 100 percent slow.

This point is so important that you'll find me repeating it often. Sorry if I bore you. I'm simply hoping to make an impression. Here's an anecdote that explains more.

Several years ago, I was teaching a beginning running class on a lovely college campus. I felt that I was doing an excellent job. I emphasised to my mostly middle-aged students that it didn't matter how slow their pace might be. Then I said it again: 'Run as slow as you can.'

Everyone nodded their comprehension, so I sent them off on several loops of a large, grassy field. Each runner was doing a personalised walk-run routine, exactly as described in these pages. I watched approvingly from the centre of the field.

For some reason, I decided to move to the edge of the loop. Now I could observe everyone up close as they chugged past. I could hear them breathe. And they were huffing and puffing much louder than I expected.

Slightly alarmed, I stopped the runners one by one on their next lap, and reached for a wrist to count their pulse. Heart rates don't lie. It turned out all my beginners were running too hard, with heart rates twenty to thirty beats per minute higher than they should have been. As beginners, they didn't understand what slow, relaxed running should feel like.

I knew I needed a new, more drastic strategy. For a moment I was flummoxed. Then a crazy idea popped into my head. What if I were to run in front of each of my students?

One at a time, I gave it a try. As each runner approached me, I jumped in front of him or her, and ran there for several minutes as we chugged around the loop. I ran really, really slow – the way I wanted them to run.

At first, they tripped on my heels several times. Then they adjusted. They couldn't believe how slow we were going. In fact, several protested. 'You sure it's okay to run this slow?' they asked. 'It seems a little ridiculous.'

But it wasn't. It was just right. Soon they stopped protesting, stopped huffing and puffing, and began to actually enjoy their run.

**Do the runner's shuffle:** Some runners have long, flowing strides. Others shuffle along, barely lifting their knees as they advance one foot in front of the other. Flowing may sound more aesthetically pleasing, but a shuffle is more efficient.

Here's how to do the shuffle. Don't think about lifting your knees high and extending your front foot far ahead of your body. Instead, let the foot fall back to the ground again as soon as it's ready. This will give you an economical stride that's well suited to slow running.

**Run backwards:** Honest. I'm not kidding. Turn around and run backwards for just a few yards. You'll naturally run with a short stride (to protect yourself from losing balance and falling over), and you'll also land on the front part of your foot. Pay attention to the 'feel' of this stride. Then turn around again, and run the same way going forward.

You don't have to continue landing on your forefeet. Transition to a relaxed heel strike. But keep your stride short and soft.

**Not a moral failing:** Beginning runners often don't run as slow as they should because they feel guilty about it. They feel there is something wrong – almost morally wrong – about running so slow. Aren't we always supposed to give our best?

Well, yes. Ultimately we all want to do the best we can in any activity or profession. But running presents a clear case of the end justifying the means. To get fitter, healthier, and maybe even faster, you have to do a lot of slow running. Especially when you're just starting out.

To prevent yourself from going too fast, try this. Imagine that I'm running in front of you with a big 'Slow down' sign on my back. And don't step on my heels.

# 4

# The Power of Two: Walking + Running

ALL SUCCESSFUL BEGINNING running programmes follow a walk-run routine. Sometimes it's called a run-walk, or even a run-walk-run. It doesn't matter. There's no reason to quibble. All these terms mean basically the same thing. So let's get going.

Walk-run plans are the right starting point because they are simple, safe, progressive, flexible, and proven. They work for a wide range of individuals, relatively young to relatively old, fit and healthy to not-quite-there-yet. Most importantly, you can tailor a walk-run plan to your personal needs, no matter your age, weight, current exercise activity, or lack thereof.

How does a walk-run plan work? First you walk. Then you run. Then you stop running, and begin walking again. Then you run again. Couldn't be easier.

Most beginners can continue like this for 30 minutes. In fact, that should be your goal. I realise 30 minutes might sound like a lot. However, if you don't suffer from serious heart disease or another chronic illness, it's very attainable. Trust me on this one. I've seen people do it.

Here's the thing, though. It's only doable if you make two smart choices at the outset. First, select the right walk-run ratio. Second, run slooooow while you're running. Speed kills. Don't let it ruin your first days of running.

On page 19, I've outlined a basic Beginning Walk-Run Programme. Please understand: This isn't meant to be the best programme for everyone. It will be too easy for some, and too difficult for others. I only want to give you an example of the format of the programme – how the days and weeks fit together, and the gradual progression of walk-run minutes.

If you find it too difficult to run for 15 seconds of each minute in week one, that's no problem. Switch to just 5 seconds of running. Your first walk-run week will then be 55-5 instead of 45-15. The second week, you can progress to 50-10. And so on.

On the other hand, if you're ready to run for 2 minutes at a time, you can go straight to Week 7 of my sample programme. You'll finish the programme in ten weeks instead of sixteen. Nicely done!

**Take your time:** Whatever plan you design for yourself, take your time. Patience is an essential quality for beginning runners. Go slow and enjoy the exciting process of getting in shape. Take as long as you need to reach the point where you run continuously for 30 minutes.

If you get sick or injured or encounter other obstacles, drop back several weeks, and pick up from there. Make each workout as comfortable as can be. The goal is never to increase your pace. The goal is always to stay relaxed. It might seem a miracle, but you'll get both fitter and faster even as the runs grow easier.

**Keep it going:** The last half of the programme looks more difficult than the first. It's not. That's one of the beauties of running. Once you get 'over the hump' of the first four to six weeks, you'll find it relatively simple to add ever-larger chunks of running.

Suddenly your legs and lungs are more accustomed to running. It becomes second nature, like a stroll around the block. This is a great time to slap yourself on the back for coming so far. But don't get greedy. Don't try to go too fast or too far. Stick with the plan.

**Aim for a new goal:** The beginners plan ends when you reach 30 minutes of controlled, relaxed running. There's a good reason for this. All national and world fitness guidelines recommend 150 minutes of moderate aerobic exercise a week. That's the level associated with major health enhancements, including significantly lower levels of heart disease, diabetes, hypertension, cancer, and depression.

So if good health is all you want from your running (and it's plenty!), you don't ever need to do more than 30 minutes at a time, three to five times a week, depending on how much other activity you get. The idea is to hit 150 minutes. For fitness, it doesn't have to be just running.

But if you do just run, you can, in fact, do less. Exercise science experts have established that running counts as 'vigorous' activity, no matter how slow you might be. And when it comes to vigorous exercise, you only need 75 minutes a week. That's the bonus that running gives you versus walking. Minute per minute, it's essentially twice as healthy.

Still, there are many good reasons for going longer than 30 minutes. Do you crave more challenge, excitement, and self-exploration in your life? An even more optimal health? To many of us, these are important considerations. Move onward and upward if you feel the urge.

# Sample Walk-Run Plan for Beginning Runners

Do each walk-run three times during the week. See page 16 for how to customise this plan.

*Week 1:* Walk 45 seconds, run 15 seconds. Repeat 29 times.

*Week 2:* Walk 40 seconds, run 20 seconds. Repeat 29 times.

*Week 3:* Walk 30 seconds, run 30 seconds. Repeat 29 times.

*Week 4:* Walk 20 seconds, run 40 seconds. Repeat 29 times.

*Week 5:* Walk 15 seconds, run 45 seconds. Repeat 29 times.

*Week 6:* Walk 10 seconds, run 50 seconds. Repeat 29 times.

*Week 7:* Walk 1 minute, run continuously for 2 minutes. Repeat 9 times.

*Week 8:* Walk 1 minute, run continuously for 3 minutes. Repeat 7 times.

*Week 9:* Walk 1 minute, run continuously for 4 minutes. Repeat 5 times.

*Week 10:* Walk 1 minute, run continuously for 5 minutes. Repeat 4 times.

*Week 11:* Walk 1 minute, run continuously for 6 minutes. Repeat 3 times.

*Week 12:* Walk 1 minute, run continuously for 8 minutes. Repeat 3 times.

*Week 13:* Walk 1 minute, run continuously for 10 minutes. Repeat 2 times.

*Week 14:* Walk 1 minute, run continuously for 12 minutes. Repeat 1 time; followed by walk 1 minute, run 3 minutes.

*Week 15:* Walk 1 minute, run continuously for 14 minutes. Repeat 1 more time.

*Week 16:* Run continuously for 30 minutes.

# 5

# The Running Habit

VETERAN RUNNERS DON'T have to think about their next run, or plan very much for it. They just do it. Running has become a habit for them, much like teeth-brushing, eating three meals, and going to work Monday to Friday.

Irregular runners, on the other hand, spend more time thinking and plotting than doing. They conjure up half a dozen questions that must be answered before a run. Am I hydrated enough? Should I buy new shoes first? Where's my GPS watch? Do I have any dry shorts? And so on.

Members of the latter type find that every run seems to disrupt their day. They haven't yet learned to make running into a habit – something that is second nature, like buying milk for the kids every time you go to the supermarket.

Fortunately, the science of healthy habit formation has made significant progress in recent years. In a 2012 journal article titled 'Making Health Habitual', three British psychologists laid out the four steps they have found most successful.

Here are the steps:

1) Decide on a goal.
2) Choose a simple, daily action that will help you achieve your goal.
3) Plan a consistent time and place when you will complete your

daily action.

4) Every time you find yourself at the chosen time and place, do the action.

Many habit experts also suggest the following practices: Write down your goal, and put it in a place you will see every day. Start simple. Commit to at least thirty days. Enlist the help of family, friends, or social media contacts. Lastly and most importantly, get started. There is great power in starting.

Most of us are familiar with the old Chinese proverb: 'A journey of a thousand miles begins with a single step.' So it is with a beginning running programme. Similarly, when author-speaker-beginning runner John 'The Penguin' Bingham started his fitness journey, he noted: 'The miracle isn't that I finished. The miracle is that I had the courage to start.'

Yes, it takes courage. Yes, you can do it. Just get started.

**Run at the same time every day:** You brush your teeth and go to work at the same time every day. Your running needs a regular time as well. Many runners prefer the morning, before their daily 'To Do' list expands to an unmanageable length. Also, morning runners report that they feel better and more productive all day long.

Lunch is the second-best time. Skip a heavy meal, and head out for 40 minutes with several co-workers. You can eat a whole-grain sandwich and yogurt back at your desk. Can't fit in a run until after work? So be it. Better late than never.

**Establish a ready-set-go routine:** This is what the British researchers meant when they outlined their time-place-action system. Sit for 5 minutes with a cup of coffee – morning, noon, or night – and then do your run. Substitute tea or sparkling water – just as good. I like to meditate for 5 minutes before running. I have friends who do several yoga poses before they run. Pick your own routine. Set the stage first, then head out the door.

**Reward yourself:** You're not a rat in a cage, but … well, you are a little like a rat in a cage. We all crave rewards for a new habit. The experts agree on this, and the research results are consistently supportive.

There are many great ways to reward yourself after a run, and two bad ones. The bad ones are eating an unhealthy, high-sugar-and-fat treat, or reclining on your sofa for the rest of the day. Avoid both.

Instead, be creative with your rewards, and make them personally meaningful. My wife likes to sing and prance around the house after a run, declaring herself a goddess of the highest order. Then she fills her appointment book with half a dozen gold stars to showcase her glimmering brilliance. Me? I'm more understated. I like to put a few key numbers in my training log, so I can add them up at the end of the week, month, and year.

I have friends who put a dollar in a jar after every run, and save up for a special purpose. Some runners make 'commitment contracts' on the internet. You can even pledge funds to a charity or political group you don't like. You'll have to give them money if you don't succeed in your new habit. Some research indicates that 'negative reinforcement' is stronger than positive reinforcement. Whatever works for you.

# 6

# Women's Running

WOMEN ARE BETTER runners than men. I say this all the time: when speaking at running seminars, when interviewed on radio and TV, and especially when training with favourite female running partners. It never hurts to solidify bonds with those all-important running buddies.

Here's what I don't mean and do mean. I don't mean that women are faster than men, or will eventually beat men. That's not going to happen. Men have a physiological advantage based on their higher testosterone levels. On average, the world's fastest men are about 10 percent faster than the best women.

At the same time, the best women beat 99 percent of all men. And there are lots of very fast, very strong women who excel in the mile, the marathon, and even longer race distances. Men had a substantial, historic head start over women in running (and all sports), but women have been making, and continue to make incredible strides.

They particularly shine when we look at participation levels. In 1960, there were almost no female distance runners. A decade later, there were only a handful. Today, however, women make up more than half the total running population. They have surpassed men. Given the right opportunity, they quickly embrace fitness and health habits.

That's one reason why women make better runners than men. But how did this remarkable revolution take place? It happened because women have an abundance of the talents and characteristics central to success in running: discipline, determination, goal-setting, organisation, time management, listening, life balance, keeping things in perspective, and understanding how small steps can lead eventually to great achievements.

These same skills also make women great mothers. And partners. And employees. And artists. And scientists. And friends. And CEOs. And much more.

I learned this for sure when researching a prior book, *First Ladies of Running*, about the pioneers who launched the women's running boom fifty years ago. The First Ladies had tremendous courage, of course. They needed it to buck regulations that prevented women from entering road races with men.

They faced a bigger barrier in the world of social-cultural myths. In the 1950s and 1960s, many self-proclaimed experts asserted that women who played sports would turn into mannish, muscle-bound Neanderthals. Many physicians pronounced that running long distances would damage 'the female organs', preventing future pregnancy and normal childbirth.

But the First Ladies of Running refused to be deterred. They felt so free and natural when running that they just knew it had to be a healthy activity. And they had dreams, just like men. They wanted to challenge themselves and learn how far they could go. It turned out to be a very great distance indeed.

**Follow the recipe:** One reason women excel at running is because they follow the recipe for beginning runners. Men often charge into running like the proverbial bull in a china shop. They break the rules. Testosterone running amok leads to setbacks, injuries, and discouragement.

Women, at least in my experience, understand the value of following the guidelines and getting things right – the right proportions, the right timing, and the right recovery periods. They don't try to set personal records every day. They focus on the long-term view.

**Listen to your body:** Men ignore the symptoms. Women tune into them, and take appropriate action. Medical surveys have shown that women are up to three times as likely to consult a physician when something's wrong.

In running, this kind of attentiveness and vigilance pays off over and over. Often it's as simple as resting for three days when you feel an early ankle pain. Or taking 10 minutes to apply an ice pack to a sore knee rather than rushing out to mow the lawn.

**Pair up. Double the fun:** Women love to get together with their friends for what was once called a coffee morning. Now it's more likely a group run. And virtually nothing is more instrumental to continued running success than several trustworthy training partners.

You can't miss your workouts when others are waiting. There's too much gossip to be shared. Of course, women run hard when they're feeling competitive. They often travel together to favourite half-marathons to attack their personal records. But on day-to-day social runs, they have no trouble slowing down enough to accommodate the slowest member of their group. Women follow the 'talk test' rule: Run comfortably enough to carry on a normal conversation.

# 7

# The Best Shoe For You

MOST OF THE time, I'd be the last person to tell you to spend money on running equipment. You're more likely to hear me say, 'There are a lot of cool gizmos and gadgets, but . . .' Who needs them? They don't actually help you run. They just divert your attention.

If you ask me, less equipment is often better. I believe the more attention you pay to your running, from your breathing, to your foot strike, to the kaleidoscopic thoughts that flit through your mind, the better.

Running shoes are another matter. They make a difference. The right shoes can dramatically improve your running. Or unravel it. Don't squander your money on other doodads. Buy a decent pair of shoes.

Which running-shoe brand? Nike, Adidas, Asics, Puma, Brooks, New Balance, Saucony, Mizuno, Under Armour? (And there are many others.) It doesn't matter. There are more running shoe companies on the market now than ever before, and all of them make good shoes. Don't worry about brand names. You just have to try several until you find the one that works best for you.

Here's what to look for. First, don't buy a pair of flimsy, super-lightweight 'barefoot' or 'minimalist' shoes. A few years back, these were all the rage, boosted by Chris McDougall's rousing tale, *Born To Run*, about the almost-mythic Tarahumara Indians of Mexico's Copper Canyon. They run prodigious distances in crude huaraches fashioned from discarded car tyres and a couple of leather straps.

Now the pendulum has swung back from that extreme – a good thing, I believe. I favour 'natural' eating and running as much as the next person, but few runners (and even fewer beginners) do well with super-lightweight shoes.

You don't want to run in heavy, stiff, almost-military-grade hikers. However, you do want to give your feet some, but not too much, cushioning and protection. Your ankles, knees, and hips will thank you.

**Choose comfort first:** In 2015, a Canadian researcher who has spent more time reviewing runner biomechanics and running shoes than anyone else, published a groundbreaking paper in the *British Journal of Sports Medicine*. Benno Nigg's report reached a surprising conclusion: Runners should mostly ignore all the gimmicks and devices that manufacturers build into their running shoes. And then advertise heavily.

Instead, Nigg advises, opt for the most comfortable shoes you can find. You might suppose that comfort represents a completely subjective, non-scientific, and confusing judgment. Nigg sees things differently. To him, comfort is the end result of your brain, legs, and feet communicating with each other on a high-IQ level.

'When selecting a running shoe, the athlete should select a comfortable product using his/her own comfort filter,' Nigg concluded. 'This automatically reduces the injury risk.'

**Shop at a speciality running store:** Yes, this means you must buck the trend. Running shoes might cost a bit less when ordered online, but nothing can match the retail experience. First, and very importantly, you'll get to try on three or four different pairs of shoes. This will allow you to make the Nigg 'comfort' comparison.

Second, when you shop at a speciality running store staffed by experienced local runners, you'll be able to pick their brains. What new models have recent customers liked the most? Which is the best shoe for a beginner? For a heavy runner? For answers like these and other important questions, no one can match veteran retailers who work with hundreds of customers.

**Ignore the jargon:** The running shoe world is full of tech talk. At almost every turn, you'll encounter terms like 'pronation', 'supination', 'arch height', 'heel to toe drop', 'midsole foam', 'orthotics', and many more.

Don't obsess about these terms, and don't be swayed by them. Buy the shoes – not too thin, and not too thick – that feel most comfortable, flexible, and supportive. The right pair will give you the sense they were custom created for you by an old-world craftsman.

For decades, running books and magazines recommended the 'wet test' – stepping into a pan of water, then onto a dry surface to create an outline of the bottom of your foot – to help you find the shoes that functioned best with your arch type – high, medium, or flat. Then, in 2010, the US Marine Corps actually tested this protocol. It reported: 'Assigning shoe based on the shape of the plantar foot surface [arch type] had little influence on injuries.'

Trust yourself.

# 8

# Flat And Fabulous

THE WORLD IS full of fantastic, undulating landscapes. Ultimately, running over such terrain can add to your thrill and excitement. At the starting line of your journey, however, it's much smarter to stay on the flatlands.

The best distance runners in the world, the Kenyans, do an inordinate amount of their running on the steep slopes of the Rift Valley. This training gives them lean, muscular legs, and amazing aerobic power. It leads to marathon victories in places like Boston, New York, Chicago, London, Berlin, and other major events around the globe.

Kenyans excel in hill-running because they have been trekking up and down hills from the day they learned to walk. You haven't. As a beginner, don't mimic the Kenyans.

Uphill running stresses the leg muscles, forcing them to contract extra hard to lift you against the pull of gravity. This produces one of the absolute best forms of aerobic training. Elsewhere in *Run Forever*, I'll suggest you run hills. But not now.

Hill running presents a double-edged challenge. Once you reach the top, things get worse. As you turn downhill, the road shock transmitted up your body with each foot strike is greatly multiplied. Now you're running faster, with gravity, using longer strides. This increases the strain on the ankles, knees, and hips – a runner's most vulnerable joints.

Downhill running also forces the muscles to contract 'eccentrically', producing many microtears. The day after the Boston Marathon (which has a number of long, steep downhills), Boston is filled by stiff-moving runners who must turn around and walk backwards when descending stairs.

You may run Boston one day, in which case you'll have plenty of pride to alleviate the pain. When just starting out, however, you should avoid the ups-and-downs. Seek smooth, flat, stable surfaces.

Much of the time, this might be the asphalt out your front door or place of employment. Fine. Pick a flat course with as little traffic as possible, and run on the right-hand side, facing oncoming vehicles. Give them as much room as possible. Safety is always job one. Follow short loop or rectangular courses, or choose out and back routes. As your fitness increases, extend the loops, rectangles, or turnaround points.

**Hit the track:** The local high school or college track is an excellent place to run several miles. Tracks are flat, secure, beckoning, and precisely measured. Most cover 400 metres, the standard for international and Olympic racing. This means that four laps equals 1,600 metres, which is just 9 metres short of a mile. The difference is so small you can ignore it.

You might find some other beginning (or veteran) runners going through their routines on the track. Don't worry that they might scorn your slowness. Most runners are private. They will mind their own business. The extroverts will probably encourage you with a 'Nice going. You're lookin' good.'

You can give the same in return. It's always appreciated. Here's a note on track-running etiquette. If you're slower than the others, don't use the inside lanes. Run in the track's outermost three or four lanes. The inside lane is where competitive runners will be running hard intervals, and timing each lap.

**The grass is greener:** Large sports fields can offer wonderful venues for beginning runners. If they are flat enough. In the case of rugby, football, and cricket fields, they almost certainly will be. Many parents have launched their running programmes by circling the fields slowly while their kids were racing to and fro at practice or in games.

**Thumbs up for treadmills:** Serious runners used to disdain treadmills. They were ugly, clunky, expensive, and, worst of all, indoors. Real runners only ran outdoors. Preferably at 5 a.m. in a blizzard.

Thank goodness times have changed. I don't know any runners today who won't admit to the multiple advantages of occasional treadmill running. Especially at 5 a.m. in a blizzard. Or in a midsummer heatwave.

Treadmills are especially welcoming to beginning runners. You can set a comfortable speed, avoid all hills, and have no worries about extreme weather. Best of all, treadmills are soft. They 'give' a little when we run on them, unlike asphalt, concrete, and other hard surfaces. This extra cushioning might prevent injuries and/or help you during a comeback from injury.

# 9

# The Truth About Running Form

WE RUNNERS ARE naturally obsessed with our running style. We'd all like to look smoother and more symmetrical, and to run faster. Entire books have been written on how to hold your arms, head, and hips, and where and how to place your feet. If a form adjustment could nudge us forward, we'd all jump at the opportunity.

However, that magical adjustment hasn't been discovered yet. So I prefer this seemingly contradictory advice: Run tall, and run short. Run with a straight, erect carriage, and run with comfortably short strides.

Experts in the field of running biomechanics have conducted thousands of studies measuring every conceivable angle, force curve, and pace. They've looked at heel runners (the vast majority of us), forefoot runners, and everything in between. Yet they still can't tell us: This is the best way to run.

It's easy to collect massive amounts of eyeball evidence. Go to any big road race, and you can observe literally tens of thousands of runners at once. What do they share in common? Nothing. They come from both sexes, and a bewildering range of ages and body sizes.

Some look like Olympic gods when they run. Most don't. They lumber along with their legs, arms, and shoulders twisting in a sometimes bizarre manner. Still, they trundle down the road, up the hills, and across the finish line. They get the job done. It seems a mass movement miracle.

And it is. I have a good friend who always strikes me as someone who's running drunk.

His body quivers and lurches. The first time I met him at a group run, I thought: What the heck is going on with Dave? Then he took off down the road faster than I could go.

Turns out Dave suffered a massive, almost fatal stroke in the middle of a triathlon a decade ago. He has never fully recovered, and may never. But he doesn't let that stop him. He keeps in great shape, and recently completed the Boston Marathon in under 4:30.

Other runners have leg-length differences, knee replacements, or an artificial leg. Some have one arm. None move with the grace of a ballet dancer. My training partners say I have a stiff, choppy stride. I've never let it bother me.

Runners come in all shapes and sizes, and they all figure out how to get the job done. Physiology studies have shown that we have a computer on board. In other words, our body learns our most efficient way to run, and that becomes our norm. There are only a few key principles.

**Run straight and tall:** Don't slouch, and don't lean forward excessively. Ideally, your head should line up with your shoulders, your shoulders with your hips, and your hips with your feet. Some believe a small forward lean is advantageous. Okay, fine. But keep it slight, and don't lean from the hips. Lean in a straight line from the ankles upward.

Too much lean, or leaning from the hips, will prove counterproductive. You might hear some self-appointed expert claim that a big forward lean will let 'gravity do the work for you'. Wrong. Don't do it.

**Run with a comfortably short stride:** This is important. The biggest running-form mistake a beginner can make is an over-stride. Sure, it seems reasonable that a long stride would help you run farther and faster. But it won't. Quite the opposite, it will make you less efficient, and perhaps lead to injuries.

Note the deliberate language, 'comfortably short'. This is different from 'comically short'. You don't want to run with the shortest-possible stride. You want a stride that feels natural, controlled, and unforced, like a gently-flowing stream.

**Turn, turn, turn:** A comfortably short stride will also deliver a quick turnover, or stride frequency. Olympic research long ago discovered that the gold medallists run with a stride count of about 180 strides per minute. You'd do the same if you were running sub-5-minute miles, as they are.

But you're not, so your best stride frequency will likely fall in the range of 160 to 170 strides per minute. If you fall under 160, you're over-striding. Shorten your stride, and concentrate on moving your feet more quickly. This also prevents excessive bounce, another wasteful running habit.

# 10

# Relaxed Running

WE RUN PRIMARILY with our feet and legs, of course. But the upper-body appendages – shoulders, arms, hands – also play an important role. They can be tense and jerky, which tends to have the same effect on the legs. Or they can be smooth and powerful, helping to guide the legs in a similar pattern.

Many runners I know have a fascination with seeing themselves in a mirror. (I confess: I'm a charter member of this group.) It's not that we're vain. We don't expect a chiselled, cover-model reflection in the glass. We just want to check out how we look when we're running.

We take this compulsion with us from the treadmills at the local health club to a famous plate-glass window at the 6.5-mile mark of the Boston Marathon. While chugging past this window, Boston runners always edge toward it, and sneak a peek over their right shoulder. How am I lookin'?

All veteran runners aim to cover ground in as relaxed a manner as possible. The less strain you carry with you on the run, the farther and easier you can go. The enemy is tenseness.

Relaxation begins with the face. If you scowl, you'll run slow, tense, and huffy. On the other hand, I've actually read studies showing that a relaxed and smiling face improves running economy. The brain of course senses what your face is doing. When you smile, it interprets this as a feeling-good input. It thinks that if you're feeling good, you must be ready to run strong.

The hands also make a major contribution to your running relaxation. You can't run smooth with a fist that's balled up into a boxer's clenched weapon, or with a hand that's flopping from the wrist as if cleaved by a butcher's knife.

Instead, aim to run as if carrying an uncooked egg in both hands. You have to grasp the egg firmly enough that it can't slip through your fingers, and crash to the ground. But also lightly enough not to crush it in your hands, producing a gooey mess of yolk and eggshell.

I've never actually seen anyone running with eggs in their hands, but I love the imagery. It totally works. You could give it a try, or you could simply walk around the house for a few minutes with an egg in each hand to get the right feel.

At any rate, the goal is to run with your fingers loosely cupped together, the thumb resting on top. When you master this hand position, your arms and shoulders should fall naturally into an economical, back-and-forth rhythm.

**Drop your shoulders:** To keep your shoulders loose and comfortable, let them drift to a relaxed, low position. Don't hunch your shoulders up high as if trying to reach your ears. That just increases the tension to your neck, back, and arms. Drop your shoulders low as if holding your dog on a leash while walking her around the block.

When you run with relaxed hands and shoulders, your upper body naturally assumes an easy, symmetrical flow. It doesn't waste any of the energy being produced by your legs, the 'engine' of your running. You run smooth and powerful.

**Tuck your elbows in:** Holding your elbows close to your body at all times will improve your economy. When your elbows stray from your sides, your hands and shoulders are also likely to flail. Again, excess arm movement leads to wasted energy.

**Don't punch the air:** Sometimes I see runners who look like they're punching the air with their arms and hands. To tell the truth, I mostly encounter this oddity in TV commercials and magazine advertisements. For some reason, the ad wizards on Madison Avenue believe that runners should employ a hyper-energetic pumping motion with their arms.

The reality, of course, is quite the opposite. Great runners don't waste energy with their arms. They want all effort to go to the legs. This was made remarkably clear when Nike organised a sub-2-hour marathon attempt in 2017.

The winner of that highly publicised attempt, Eliud Kipchoge, ran a remarkable 2:00:26. Watching him, the first thing you noticed was the lack of arm-pumping in front of his chest. It made him look effortless – the very point of efficient running.

## 11

# Safety First: No Headphones

LISTEN, I'M SORRY. I know you like listening to tunes while you run, so you're not going to be happy with this rule. You think you need the music to distract and entertain you while you run. You can't imagine going 30 minutes without The Rolling Stones or Bruce Springstein or your favourite group that I've never heard of.

And I'm willing to lighten up on this dictum eventually. Maybe in a few months when you're running more confidently and relaxed. Maybe if you're running on a treadmill or a well-travelled route. Maybe when you're trying to extend your run to an hour or more.

But not now – not when you are just starting out. Now you should be listening to your environment, your body, and all the other sounds around you. First and foremost, listen for cars, cyclists, pedestrians, and everything else that could affect your safety. That's the first and most important rule of running: Safety first.

Headphones don't just funnel sounds to your ears. They also diminish your attention to other input – sensory data brimming with valuable information that's important to runners.

For example, your breathing warns you if you are running too fast. The sweat on your brow signals possible dehydration. When your ears and mind drift too deep into the audio zone, you might react slower to the bicyclist speeding your way. Or the crack in the pavement. Or the pothole in the road.

You'll also miss the richness of sounds in the natural world around you. I'm thinking here about such miracles as crickets, birds, the frogs of spring, the honking, southward-seeking geese of autumn and winter, the crunch of soft snow, the rustling leaves, the wind whistling through treetops, the lashing rain when a sudden storm catches you by surprise, a friend's wistful tale of her adoption, your child's complaints about a school teacher, the voice in your own head hoping for more peace, prosperity, and understanding across the globe.

And these are just the smallest percent of what you'll encounter on the road. I've experienced all of these. You will too. And many more – especially the ones most germane to your own life and world.

**Boost your creativity:** Hundreds of authors, musicians, and artists have attested to the creativity they gain from their regular running routines. Prolific novelist and short-story writer Joyce Carol Oates once wrote about this for *The New York Times*. She began her essay: 'Running! If there's any activity happier, more exhilarating, more nourishing to the imagination, I can't think what it might be.'

The acclaimed Japanese author Haruki Murakami wrote a book titled *What I Talk About When I Talk About Running*. Quite a bit, it turned out. Many of the ideas came to him spontaneously. 'I usually run with my mind empty,' he told *Runner's World*. 'However, when I run empty-minded, something naturally and abruptly crawls in sometime.'

To me, this is one of the things I most enjoy about running. I never know what's going to come to me. Running often delivers surprising insights.

**Open conversation:** When runners get together, whether just two at a time or many at one time, the conversation seems to flow with unusual ease. A psychologist friend of mine has suggested we feel freer and less inhibited when we run. Something loosens within us.

Another theory holds that it's easier to talk about things when you aren't looking into someone's eyes. We run side by side, eyes glued ahead. No one's staring at anyone else the way we do across a dinner table or living room.

I only know this. The most serious discussions I have ever had, and the most honest – about love, death, miscarriage, children, divorce, financial fears, and the like – have occurred when I was running with a friend. Open up. It's good for everyone.

**Unplug, and chill out:** Every runner recognises that regular workouts reduce stress. If we miss three or four days in a row, we begin to feel antsy and anxious. A 2013 paper in *Frontiers in Psychiatry* found the same. How does exercise reduce stress?

The paper's authors could not pinpoint one key pathway. There were many. 'No single mechanism sufficiently accounts' for the effect. Nonetheless, 'Physical activity positively impacts a number of biological, as well as psychological, mechanisms.'

Whatever the precise scientific explanation, we know the simple truth. We live in a 24/7 world that seems to spin faster every day. Running offers a blessed time-out. We can unplug and chill out. What's not to like about that?

# 12

# Post-Run Snacking Not Allowed

IN RECENT YEARS, no aspect of sports nutrition has received more coverage than post-workout recovery foods (and drinks). According to many experts, we have a 30- to 60-minute 'window' after finishing a run when the muscles are most receptive to carbohydrate foods, which are converted to glycogen in our muscles. This stored glycogen acts as fuel for the next workout.

Seems a good deal. And it's no doubt helpful if you're an Ironman triathlete or Olympic marathoner who's doing the day's second long training session in four hours. Sound like you?

I didn't think so. For the rest of us, this glycogen opportunity is more like the drive-through window at your local fast-food joint. It's just another chance – a trap, really – to consume calories we don't need.

Lose five pounds, and you'll find yourself running better every day. Gain five, and you'll struggle more. That's why the best post-run drink is a fresh, cooling glass of water. Add a little whole fruit – banana, apple, orange, if you like. Then stop. You'll get all the glycogen-supplying carbs and protein you need at your next meal in just a couple of hours.

Most of the US adult population gains one to two pounds per year. Runners do much better, by 50 percent, but still gradually gain. Besides looking bad, this midlife weight gain increases your risk of diabetes, high blood pressure, heart disease, knee and hip arthritis, depression, and even cancer.

You might think new runners should lose weight, not gain. And many do. But too many succumb to an insidious 'reward' habit. They run several miles, and then, consciously or not, feel that they deserve some tempting, high-calorie foods. When you do this, it's very easy to eat more calories than you burned while running. Waaaay easy.

Beginning runners in particular must guard against this pitfall. The calorie maths is stacked against you. So run, drink water, and wait for your next meal.

**Calories out, calories in:** Running increases your calorie burn for sure. But often not as much as you might imagine. For example, a 3-mile run burns 100 calories per mile, to use the simplest calculation. (For a far more accurate per-mile calorie-burn estimate, multiply your weight by .75. That is, if you weigh 150 pounds, you burn 112 calories per mile. If you weigh 200, you burn 150 calories per mile.)

So let's say you weigh 150 pounds, and burn 336 calories during a 3-mile run (3 x 112). Then, after your run, you decide to have a blueberry muffin and a low-fat chocolate milk. You've heard that low-fat chocolate milk is a good recovery drink. (It is!)

Only problem is that the muffin and milk amount to almost 600 calories. That's practically twice what you burned while running. No wonder the bathroom scale is headed in the wrong direction.

**Drink water first (and mostly):** The absolute smartest nutrition and weight loss strategy a beginning runner can follow is to drink water before and after running. Substitute it for what you're drinking now – soda, milk, fruit juice, even coffee and tea if you are adding sugar and cream to them.

Water is the perfect runner drink. It doesn't mess with your stomach, it doesn't add calories to your daily count, it doesn't stain your teeth or promote calories, and it's incredibly refreshing and rehydrating.

**Focus on fun:** We tend to reward ourselves after we do something difficult that requires effort and determination. On the other hand, we don't compensate in the same way if we've had fun, say by frolicking in a water park. So, if you can turn your workouts into fun runs, you'll eat healthier.

This was actually proven by a nutrition study. After a 5K race, researchers asked runners how much they had enjoyed the event. Then the runners were allowed to eat either a healthy oat bar or a not-so-healthy chocolate bar. The runners who had fun during the race were more likely to select the oat bar. Those who found the race difficult and fatiguing chose the chocolate bar.

So, on your next run, think about what a pleasant time you're having. Afterwards, focus on the fun. After all, you could have been doing something much worse, like giving a speech or reporting for an income tax review. If you think fun, you're less likely to eat badly.

# SECTION 2

# RUNNING NUTRITION

# Lab Experiments

FROM MY EARLIEST days as a runner, I've been deeply interested in the nutrition and hydration that produce peak performance. I'm not sure where this came from. Certainly not my days as a Little League baseball player.

Then I believed the best diet should meet two requirements. Before a game, I had to eat steak and baked potatoes. (In a pinch, hamburgers and French fries were an acceptable alternative.) After the game, we had to stop at Dairy Queen for a large ice cream cone.

My high-school cross-country coach, John Kelley, introduced me to a different world. He was an ovo-lacto-vegetarian. He ate eggs and dairy products, but no red meat. I first encountered wheatgerm at the Kelley breakfast table, and soon learned to enjoy its chewy texture. At seventeen, I decided that vegetarian eating held the secret to great endurance running.

What I lacked in knowledge, I made up for in stupidity. My diet was so restrictive – about 50 percent wheat cereal and milk – that I wonder how I survived. I knew almost nothing about nutrition then. Science never entered the picture. I plunged into vegetarianism with the same passion I pursued running.

Five years later, I had my first opportunity to be a running guinea pig. A young physiologist named David Costill, PhD, invited me to his lab. Costill had received a small grant to study how hydration affected distance runners. He wanted me to run a 20-miler on his treadmill on three successive days – once with no fluids, once with water, once with a new product named 'Gatorade'.

I couldn't say 'Yes' fast enough. I couldn't imagine anything more exciting than gaining scientific insight into the way my body reacted while I was running. Costill drove to Detroit, where I was competing in the NCAA indoor 2-mile championship behind the likes of superstars Jim Ryun and Gerry Lindgren (and finishing far behind them). Then we headed south through the early-morning hours to Ball State University in Muncie, Indiana.

On the next three mornings, I ran 20 miles on the Ball State treadmill at a pace just over 6:00 minutes per mile. During one run, I ran dry – with no fluids. During another, Costill and colleagues handed me a flask of water every 10 minutes, and asked me to drain it. On the third, I was handed an equal quantity of Gatorade, recently invented at Florida State University in Tallahassee, Florida.

The first couple of drinks during each run were refreshing, whether water or Gatorade. After that, I developed a queasy, sloshy feeling in my stomach. Too much already. I looked beseechingly in Costill's direction. Do I have to? He nodded, Yes. I had to keep drinking. This was science. We had to be consistent.

I grew tired from the running, sure. Ten miles. Fifteen miles. Eighteen. But the drinking was worse. I had grown accustomed, over five or six years, to running considerable distances with little or no refreshment. I had finished two Boston Marathons. Boston had no fluid stops. Now, in Costill's lab, I was growing nauseous. I started to worry that I might vomit.

The worst was still to come. After I finished each 20-miler, Costill sat me on a bench, and began to thread a narrow plastic tube up my nose, down my throat and oesophagus, and into my stomach. He needed to siphon out the contents of my stomach to determine how much fluid was left there, and hence not absorbed into my bloodstream.

I gagged. I felt like I was being suffocated. 'It's okay. Just relax,' said Costill. 'Pretend you're swallowing spaghetti.'

Oh, sure. That'll work.

While Costill was draining my stomach, his associates asked a series of questions about how I had felt during the run. They wanted to determine my RPE (Relative Perceived Exertion) during each of the three treadmill runs. I pointed to numbers on their sheet that indicated effort. This part was easy. I felt best when I drank nothing, as was my custom. And worst when I drank the Gatorade, an entirely new and foreign experience.

Later, Costill sat me down to go over the results. According to his analysis, I had performed the best (consuming less oxygen) on Gatorade and the worst while drinking nothing. In other words, the exact opposite of how I had felt subjectively during the three runs.

This brings up a very important point about sports research. Scientists are forever conducting experiments that yield results that should be associated with important health or performance outcomes. In theory. It's far more difficult, and much less common, to link the experimental condition to an *actual* health or performance benefit.

I like to say: The measure is not the thing. Costill's results did not constitute proof that I run faster with Gatorade than with nothing. In the spring of 1968, in his lab, in my first time drinking Gatorade, I could have guaranteed that would not have been the case.

One month later, on a warm day in April, I won the Boston Marathon without drinking anything en route. I weighed 138 pounds on the start line, and 129 at the finish. I know this because Costill was there to weigh me. I'm also quite sure that, if someone had given me Gatorade on the course, I wouldn't have run as well.

Through the years, I've enjoyed volunteering for other nutrition and physiology studies. Once I joined a group of runners who were consuming a diet consisting 90 percent of fats. I thought it would be yummy, like the Dairy Queen of my Little League days. Instead, after just two meals, I couldn't stand the thought of eating another plate of near-lard.

I've also run in a heat chamber cranked up to ninety degrees Fahrenheit. We wanted to see what this would do to my body temperature. No surprise, it spiked. Humans are better heat runners than shaggy, thick-haired bison, but we're still better off in the cool and shade.

Here's what science and various experiments have taught me about nutrition and performance. Don't expect miracles. Secret foods and pills won't make you faster. Only training and smart racing can do that. There is no one-and-only true path – not the vegetarian way nor vegan nor Palaeo nor any other anointed diet. Rather, there are many healthy diet patterns.

Whole carbohydrates improve performance. So does coffee/caffeine, and moderate water drinking. Use Lucozade Sport or another sports drink if you have tried it, and liked it many times. Avoid most processed foods. Eat real fruits, real vegetables, eggs, dairy, whole grains, legumes, and healthy fish, fowl, and meat.

Don't try to be perfect. Go to Nando's from time to time. It feeds the child within, which is never a bad idea.

# 1

# The Kingdom of Carbohydrates

DESPITE INTERNET FRENZIES and best-selling books to the contrary, carbohydrates are still the prime energy food for runners. Simply put, carbs supply the working muscles with the fuel they can burn most efficiently for high-intensity exercise (and all running, even slow running, qualifies as high-intensity exercise). Your body can burn fats in a pinch, and small amounts of protein, but it won't feel good when it does. And you won't perform your best.

For proof, we need look no farther than the best distance runners in the world – the East Africans. Kenyan runners have been extensively studied, as science searches to explain their astounding successes. And research into the Kenyan diet has consistently yielded the same result: The Kenyan runners eat a diet that's astonishingly high in carbohydrates. They get 70 percent or more of their energy from carbs. The typical American, by comparison, gets 50 percent of his or her calories from carbs.

Of course, low-carb, often-high-fat diets have become the rage in the US As have similar alternatives with names like the Palaeo diet, the ketogenic diet, and so on. Sugar and high-fructose corn syrup have been particularly vilified.

Well, sure, no one's arguing for the health benefits of added sugars. Avoid them as much as possible. But don't be duped by logical fallacies. Just because added sugars are bad, that does not mean that high-fat diets are good.

Quite the opposite. The vast majority of nutrition experts point out that carbohydrates continue to be the dietary mainstay of the world's healthiest populations – not just the fast Kenyans, but also the long-lived Okinawans of Japan and the thriving elders of Italy, Greece, and other Mediterranean countries.

Fruit, veggies, legumes, and whole grains – that's the ticket for runners. These foods are super healthy for several key reasons. First, they are low-fat and low-calorie. They help you maintain an optimal weight. Second, they are packed with vitamins, minerals, and antioxidants. Third, many are accompanied by soluble and insoluble fibres that are lacking in manufactured foods. Fibre has several valuable properties. It slows the absorption of sugars from the stomach, lowering the risk of high-glucose, high-insulin reaction, and it adds fullness to the meal, meaning you will stay satisfied longer and be less tempted by between-meal snacks.

**Choose clean carbs:** Years ago, I used to fill my supermarket cart with so-called 'convenience foods'. I didn't want to prepare meals at home. I wanted to spend my time training and racing. If a canned or plastic-wrapped food looked reasonably healthy, I reached for it.

Now I have a new supermarket goal. I try to go through the checkout with as few processed and pre-cooked foods as possible. I buy whole fruits, whole veggies, and big bunches of kale and lettuce. My grains, beans, nuts, seeds, and eggs are likewise unprocessed, and my Greek yogurt contains no added flavours or sweeteners. Meals take a little longer to prepare, but not much, and I enjoy the time, because I am working with low-process foods that are good for me and good for the planet.

**Aim for variety:** The greater the variety of foods you consume, the healthier your diet is likely to be. We know this because studies of people who consume vitamin and mineral supplements rarely reach the same conclusion as studies of those who eat whole foods containing supposedly-identical nutrients. Nature puts more into foods than man can extract, and inject into pills.

**You are what you do:** Many low-carb eaters avoid carbs in the belief that they lead to insulin resistance, diabetes, and weight gain. Such people follow the old 'You are what you eat' dictum. Again, there's no doubt that too much added sugar is a bad thing in anyone's diet.

However, that doesn't mean that all carbs are equally bad. An obesity expert friend of mine who has a PhD in exercise science has coined a more nuanced variation on the old catchphrase. He says, 'You are what your body does with what you eat.' More simply, you are what you do.

Here's what this means. If an overweight thirty-five-year-old consumes four slices of greasy cheese pizza, washed down with twenty-four ounces of a sugary soda, yes, he's going to nudge himself toward diabetes. But the same won't necessarily hold true for a lean thirty-five-year-old who regularly runs twenty miles a week. This person has tuned his body to deal with an occasional oversupply of fats and carbs.

You can be perfectly healthy without being perfect twenty-four hours a day.

# 2

# Healthy Fats

WHEN I BEGAN running more than fifty years ago, I tried to avoid fatty foods as much as possible. This was the era when the American Heart Association and government nutrition sources were pushing a low-fat diet. Everyone believed it was the best way to avoid heart disease. Since my grandfather had a heart attack in his fifties, and my father had a big gut with too much belly fat, I wanted to avoid a disease-causing diet. I didn't like the look of my family genetics.

But I had an even stronger reason for avoiding fatty foods: The best runners seemed to be the skinniest. Even at a time when East Africans hadn't yet climbed to the top of the marathon ladder, I could see that the guys who won big races were often the thinnest. And the ones behind were taller, wider, heavier. I wanted to win, so I forced myself onto a strict low-fat diet.

I became a vegetarian, I drank skimmed milk, I avoided eggs, and I kept a distance from junk foods. Not that I was perfect. No, I enjoyed ice cream too much for that, not to mention the German chocolate cake that my mother always baked on my birthday and other occasions.

But these were rare indulgences. The rest of the time I toed the line, and avoided high-fat foods. You could tell that with one look at me. The day that I won the Boston Marathon, I stood on the start line at 6ft 0in and 138 pounds.

No doubt I won Boston because I was one of the best-trained athletes in the field. The previous two years, I had run more than

100 miles a week almost every single week. But I also believed I won because I was among the skinniest guys on the line.

I didn't change my mind about low-fat eating for several decades. But in the early 2000s, I began to get the message. I learned that the early studies linking dietary fats to heart disease were probably flawed, and the results overstated. No, that didn't mean I could have chocolate cake and ice cream every night. But, yes, it was time for a closer look at fatty foods.

Many of them were in fact scrumptious, 100-percent natural, and health-enhancing. I started eating eggs again for the first time in decades, switched to extra virgin olive oil, regularly bought avocadoes (which thrilled my Latina wife), and increased my nut consumption. My weight stayed the same, my cholesterol profile improved, and I enjoyed my meals more.

**Avoid certain fats:** I still try to minimise my consumption of trans fats, which are largely disappearing from the American diet, and of saturated fats such as the marbling around red meats. If I see a food label with the words 'partially hydrogenated oils', I know this is code for trans fats. I put these foods back on the supermarket shelf, since trans fats have an especially pernicious effect on heart health.

As a vegetarian, I don't eat red meats. If I did, I would look for meats from free-range animals that haven't been raised on hormones. And I'd trim away as much fat as possible.

**Seek out omega-3 fats:** Populations that include regular fish consumption as a diet mainstay often have impressive records for health and longevity. Many nutritionists and epidemiologists believe this is due to the high omega-3 fatty acid content of some fish, particularly deep water fish like salmon and tuna.

In addition to possible heart-health benefits, omega-3 fats are linked with lower rates of depression. Runners will also appreciate their ability to decrease inflammation such as that associated with joint pain. You only need to eat several servings a week, and a high-quality fish oil supplement might help you get there (though supplements rarely match the benefits of real food).

Add more nuts to your diet: After I began eating more nuts in my mid-fifties, two rather remarkable things happened. First, I noticed that I was no longer hungry all day. As a result, it was easier to cut back on the large rice and pasta dishes I craved at dinner.

Even better, my blood cholesterol profile changed substantially. My 'good' HDL cholesterol almost doubled, while my 'bad' LDL cholesterol plunged. I've been eating more nuts ever since, with continued happy results.

# 3

# Muscle-Building Protein

WITH ALL THE controversies and swirling opinions over carbohydrates and fats, protein has become the lost child of the three major nutrients. That's an unfortunate result, since we all learned in junior high school that every key life process depends on proteins and amino acids.

Like everyone else, runners need plenty of protein for optimal health and maximal performance. Indeed, experts at the International Society for Sports Nutrition advise runners and other serious exercisers to consume twice as much protein per day as non-exercisers. That's because we burn many more calories on a regular basis with our running and other activities.

Also, we occasionally run tough workouts and endurance races that break down body tissues. When we follow these with protein meals, the tissues rebuild themselves even stronger. One name for this process is 'the training effect'.

In most countries around the world, no matter what the local population primarily eats, protein provides about 15 percent of total calories. Carbs and fats supply the other 85 percent, often in widely differing amounts. But the protein percentage holds steady.

This means several things. For one, you don't need a lot of protein. Nutritionists advise us to visualise meat and other protein servings the size of a tennis ball. That will do it, as long as you eat a steady supply of protein on a daily basis.

Consuming this much protein, or even a little more, may also help you lose weight or maintain a healthy weight. According to the Protein Leverage Theory, if you don't get 15 percent of your calories from protein each day, you will eat more until you do hit that amount of protein. In other words, the body is 'programmed' to eat more calories if you haven't reached your daily protein requirement.

As the obesity crisis has spread, the Protein Leverage Theory has gained more followers in the medical and nutrition communities. That's one reason you often hear the same advice: Be sure to consume some protein with every meal. When you do this, you'll be more satisfied after one meal, and less hungry at the next meal.

**Choose the best:** Animal meats provide the highest quality proteins, but too often come loaded with extra fat and calories, especially if you're a fan of fast-food burgers. Better to eat lean meats, fowl, and fish. A friend of mine, a cardiologist and medical director of the Boston Marathon, advises his patients to avoid meat from mammals. Another way of putting this: Select protein from animals that have fins and wings.

**Eat protein at every meal:** As noted, most nutritionists now recommend a modest amount of protein at every meal. That can mean milk or eggs for breakfast, yogurt or a salad with protein for lunch, and fish or Mexican food in the evening.

**Power up with non-meat proteins:** When I won the Boston Marathon in 1968, I was a vegetarian who didn't know much about vegetarian eating. At the time, there was little information for vegetarians, and few foods to choose from. Later I learned about combining complementary proteins like beans and rice. When the research favouring a Mediterranean diet began to pile up, I added salmon and occasional other fish to my diet.

Now there are many high-quality non-meat protein foods, and research has shown they don't have to be eaten together at the same meal. They can be spread throughout the day. Eggs. Low-fat dairy. Beans and lentils. Nuts. Certain grains like quinoa. Tofu and other soybean products. Cottage cheese and Greek yogurt. Vegetarians can easily meet their daily protein quota.

**Seniors:** Seek extra protein: With a growing number of over-65 citizens and citizen-athletes (like me), research into our health needs is expanding rapidly. Already, two things have become abundantly clear.

First, loss of muscle mass is a major aging problem that contributes to many falls and serious injuries. Doctors call this weakness 'sarcopenia', and it drains the health-care system, since seniors need major care after broken hips and similar injuries. Second, the decrease in muscle mass is caused by lower muscle protein synthesis among seniors. A 2016 study in *Medicine & Science in Sports & Exercise* showed that older triathletes synthesised less protein than their younger counterparts. The only way to make up for this is to increase protein consumption in your diet, and to engage in regular strength training.

# 4

# Water, the Essential Fluid

RUNNERS SWEAT A lot, and of course need to replace their sweat with fluid to stay in hydration balance. You were probably still in grade school when you first learned that humans can live far longer without food than without water. The lesson made a strong impression, so it's no wonder that you listen carefully to messages about runners and their special hydration needs. It all sounds so logical.

We live in a culture that's obsessed by fluid consumption, heavily promoted by commercial drink producers. We're almost as obsessed by fluids as we are by processed foods, also highly advertised. The difference is that we consume lots of water, an actually healthy and natural fluid. You can't say the same about processed foods. Which of them are healthy and natural?

Of course, there's a simple explanation for this difference. Coke, Pepsi, and other global corporations own a number of popular water brands. The companies are happy to market and sell bottles full of water that otherwise flow free from our household tap. Not to mention the carbonated sugar waters, sugar juices, whole juices (containing heavy doses of sugar), sports drinks, and energy drinks they also sell.

Right behind them, the coffee, tea, and beer companies are just as eager to have us consume their beverages. No wonder all the people you know seem to be sipping one fluid or another all day long. And constantly telling each other to beware the hazards of dehydration, which supposedly include headaches, fatigue, dry skin, obesity, and a nearly infinite list of imagined conditions.

Pity our poor Palaeo ancestors. How did they ever survive through long days of food gathering under a hot African sun without a litre-bottle of fluid in each hand? Oh, here's a thought.

Maybe humans are well adapted for regular, short periods of dehydration. Maybe Palaeo people drank from a stream in the morning, walked and grew dehydrated during the day, and returned to the stream at night. For about two million years before someone invented the household tap.

I grow too facetious. Here's the point. Few of us are seriously dehydrated. If we were, we'd weigh a half-pound less every morning, and that's not happening. Good hydration is absolutely essential to good running, and also ridiculously easy.

Drink water (mostly) when you are thirsty or notice your pee is yellow (rather than clear or straw-coloured). As much as possible, avoid drinks with extra sugar or fat calories. Drink alcohol with friends, and in moderation.

**Don't over-hydrate in races:** Runners once believed they should drink us much as possible in races to maximise their performance. Then, in the early 1990s, we learned that it is possible (and dangerous) to over-drink. This causes a condition called hyponatraemia, or low blood sodium, which can lead to brain swelling, and even death.

Severe hyponatraemia is rare, but occurs most often in marathons and ultramarathons, and among runners of small size (more women than men). If your stomach is sloshing or a ring is feeling unusually tight on a finger, consider these a warning sign.

Don't drink as much as you can. Don't drink at every water stop, just because you can. And don't expect water to perform miracles like relieving muscle fatigue. It can't do that. The best guideline: 'Drink when you are thirsty.'

**Follow the two-percent rule:** Recent research has shown that runners can perform their best and maintain full health up to the point of two-percent dehydration. That's quite a bit of fluid you don't have to drink while you're running. For example, a 150-pound runner can lose three pounds of water, 48 ounces, without worry. You'll run faster because you won't have to slow and walk at the water stops. You'll probably feel better as well, and suffer from fewer episodes of race nausea.

Use tried-and-true sports drinks during races: In races lasting longer than an hour, consume a sports drink for its sugars and electrolytes. You don't need sports drinks in shorter races.

In half-marathons, marathons, and other long events, grab a sports drink when you are thirsty, or on a reasonable schedule, say every 20 minutes. (More often in hot weather.) Smart, forward-thinking marathoners search out the drink that will be available at their upcoming race, and then practise with it on training runs.

# 5

# Whole Grains

RUNNERS HAVE LONG favoured pastas, breads, and rice in their diet, relying on them to provide a steady supply of high-energy carbohydrates. However, for many years, it was too easy to select processed, white grains, primarily because such foods dominated supermarket shelves. These refined grains have a high glycaemic index, especially when combined with sugar in cakes, cookies, and the like.

In other words, your body converts them rapidly to glucose. The result could be an energy rush, followed by a crash, as insulin rushes into your blood to dispose of the carbs. Not a good formula for runners.

Now there are many more choices, and nutrition-savvy athletes are switching to whole grains. For example, you can buy pastas made from red and green lentils rather than refined white flour. Brown rice is easy to find, and much tastier than white rice once you adapt to its nutty, chewy texture. Other ethnic and ancient whole grains are turning up on store shelves with increasing frequency. Some of these include quinoa (high in protein), teff (a favourite of those super-fast Ethiopian runners), freekeh, and einkorn.

Since the beginning of cross-country running in England in the 1860s, British athletes enjoyed a steaming bowl of porridge (oatmeal) for breakfast before their hares-and-hounds competitions. With modern-day milling and other manufacturing, this once-hearty breakfast changed to a soggy, mushy concoction. Today porridge is making a comeback in the form of whole-grain oatmeal. Sure, it requires a little more cooking time, but the payoff is worth the wait.

While refined grains like white rice cook faster than their whole-grain counterparts, they can't compete on the nutrition front. Whole grains include the bran (packed with fibre), the germ (vitamins, minerals, and antioxidants) and the endosperm (mostly starch). The refined, white grain contains only the endosperm, or starch. That makes it a high-glycaemic source of carbohydrate energy, but a poor source of everything else.

Whole grains get high marks for their ability to extend athletic endurance. This follows from their slow digestion, which delivers a steady stream of energy to the blood and muscles. No wonder they are favoured by many runners, especially marathoners, who have come to rely on whole grains as a high-test fuel for the long run.

**Burn more calories coming and going:** Impressive new research from Tufts University in early 2017 heralded more reasons to eat whole grains. In a well-controlled study, researchers fed subjects either 800 calories a day of refined grains or 800 calories of whole grains. Those on the whole-grain diet gained an additional 40+ calories a day of basic metabolic burn. In addition, they eliminated an extra 50+ calories daily, thanks to the high-fibre content of whole grains.

All told, the change in energy balance was worth about a five pound weight loss (over the course of a year), according to the investigators. In this particular study, the Tufts researchers didn't even measure the nutritional benefits of whole grains. They didn't have to. That has been so well established, it's a given.

When I asked about this, they responded quickly. 'We should also remember that whole grains in the diet are associated with lower cancer rates, so they're good for long-term health,' said the head investigator.

**Lose even more weight:** Other studies have also shown that whole grains can contribute to weight-loss efforts. A study in *Public Health*

*Nutrition* found that people who consume at least three servings a day of whole grains have a lower BMI (body mass index) and less belly fat than subjects eating fewer whole grains. Increased belly fat (also called visceral fat) is a leading indicator of the so-called metabolic diseases, including diabetes, that often result from overweight and obesity.

**Beat heart disease and cancer:** In 2016, the *British Medical Journal* reported that a review of studies linking whole-grain consumption and mortality produced striking results. Those who ate three one-ounce portions of whole grains per day were rewarded by a 22 percent lower risk of death from cardiovascular diseases. Whole grains also lowered death rates from cancer. A separate investigation of 17,000 Spanish adults documented a lower risk of heart disease over ten years. The benefit was strongest in those who had the highest ratio of wholegrains to total carbs in their diet.

# 6

# Food Frequency and Timing

OUR GREAT GRANDPARENTS didn't have any trouble figuring out when to eat. They sat down at regular intervals during the day to consume predictable meals. There really wasn't any other alternative. They had dozens of jobs to perform around the farm, fields, and animals.

A few years later, many had transitioned to the factory floor, which demanded constant physical labours. No one carried around plastic bags full of processed, pre-wrapped convenience snacks to munch on constantly. A meal was a serious, sit-down affair: breakfast (a big one), lunch, dinner. Following this rigid schedule, our great-grandparents were notably leaner and stronger than nearly all of their descendants fifty to seventy years later – you and me.

Nowadays we snack more or less constantly throughout the day, while also spending most of our time in a car, chair, or sofa. The result – gradual weight gain – couldn't be more predictable.

In an attempt to break this pernicious cycle, nutritionists and others have investigated various meal-timing strategies. It turns out, no surprise, that regular meals on a regular schedule are a good thing, as are gaps between meals without snacking. Consistent movement during the day stimulates muscle, and helps the body burn calories. Sitting most of the day, on the other hand, turns those calories into fat.

We have long been told that breakfast is the day's most important meal, and much research supports the role of regular breakfast consumption. One recent study showed that those who eat breakfast cereal with milk every morning are 31 percent less likely to be overweight or obese than those who skip breakfast.

The protein in milk may be the key. Protein is the nutrient that has disappeared from many breakfasts, replaced by processed, high-carb 'ready to go' foods too often consumed in the car or at your desk. In early 2017, the American Heart Association released a comprehensive, twenty-seven-page 'Scientific Statement' on meal timing and frequency. One of its strongest recommendations was to eat a healthy breakfast that included quality proteins.

**Don't graze constantly:** The idea that one should snack on foods every couple of hours throughout the day has long been a popular notion. Proponents claimed that it would keep you energised, and prevent big splurges at mealtimes, thus curtailing weight gain. However, research has failed to support this claim.

Instead, grazing provides too many opportunities to eat, so it leads to weight gain rather than weight loss. You'll do better to focus on regular, healthy meals. If you do get hungry for the occasional between-meal snack, be prepared. Have a handful of nuts nearby, or a yogurt, or whole fruit. Try to avoid the processed foods in the nearby convenience store or vending machine.

**Stop eating after dinner time:** Many of us recognise the trap of late-evening food consumption. There are just so many possibilities, whether you're enjoying social time with friends at a restaurant or bar, or relaxing at home while watching your favourite TV shows. Too often, we crave evening-time desserts laden with fats and sugars.

The night-eating routine leads to almost certain weight gain and related health concerns. Men who wake up at night to raid the refrigerator have a 55 percent increased risk of heart disease. On the other hand, one study showed that subjects who moved 300 calories a day from dinner to breakfast (without changing their total daily intake) managed a substantial weight loss. The Heart Association statement recommended that we eat during fewer hours each day, and give our bodies an ample overnight 'fast' for the important metabolic processes that take place at night.

**Try intermittent fasting:** Somewhat to my surprise, the Heart Association also found preliminary but promising results for intermittent fasting. The most popular of these diets advocates eating substantially less than normal two days a week, or every other day. Early results show that subjects don't consume enough calories during their eating days to make up for the non-eating days. Since they therefore consume fewer total calories per week, they gradually lose weight.

For runners, this pattern has a familiar ring to it. We also train in on/off days, usually referring to them as 'hard' days and 'easy' days. While I haven't seen any studies on combined eating-and-training patterns, I can imagine that they would prove complementary. Runners could eat more on hard days when they need the energy, and less on recovery days when they are not exercising so vigorously.

# 7

# Tea and Coffee

MY EARLIEST LONG runs were always followed by hot tea with a dollop of honey and milk. This was the tradition in John J. Kelley's home, and what he did, I did. Kelley embraced all weather. In winter, he particularly enjoyed pitting himself against slanting snow and frigid, penetrating winds. I often returned to his kitchen with frozen hands, toes, nose, ears, and other body parts. Fortunately, Kelley's wife, Jacintha, always had a pot of tea ready. It usually took two before my extremities began to thaw a bit.

At this point in my life (eighteen to twenty-two), I didn't even drink coffee. Tea was my first and favourite hot drink. I figured it was also a solid performance beverage. In the 1950s and 1960s, a fair number of the world's best distance runners came from England. Roger Bannister, Jim Peters, and Ron Hill were just a few. They trained in cold damp conditions, drank tea to rehydrate and replenish themselves, and then broke records from the mile to the marathon. If tea was good enough for them, it was good enough for me.

Decades later, I would travel to the Rift Valley of Kenya, land of the current world's top runners. Many hillsides were covered by tea fields, since Kenya had been colonised by the British, and the Kenyan runners drank amazing quantities of hot tea all day long. They drank tea before running, after running, and while sitting around and not running. Kenyans prepare tea that's super-sweet, heated with milk already in the huge cooking pot, and so steamy that I couldn't put it to my lips until it had cooled for several minutes.

As for coffee, in the early 1970s, exercise physiologist David Costill, PhD, published research showing that it improves performance. This made coffee all the rage among marathoners. Several decades later, another friend and physiologist, Lawrence Armstrong, PhD, discovered that moderate coffee drinking has no diuretic effect. His report overturned the conventional thinking.

**Don't worry about coffee alarmists:** Coffee is a worldwide beverage, and therefore one whose health effects have been researched in many large population studies. Sure, some people are hypersensitive, and everyone should avoid high-calorie coffee drinks with lots of sugar and cream. But the most recent and biggest coffee studies have linked it to positive health outcomes, particularly lower rates of diabetes and all-cause mortality. It also reduced depression rates and cognitive decline.

In a 2015 report in *Circulation*, investigators tracked three large subject groups for an amazing 4,690,000 person-years of follow-up. Subjects who consumed up to five cups of coffee a day enjoyed an 8 to 15 percent lower rate of total mortality during the study period than non-drinkers. Coffee had no effect, good or bad, on cancer deaths. The lower mortality came from decreased heart deaths, brain diseases, and suicide.

**Drink your antioxidants:** What makes coffee a good-for-you beverage? You've probably read dozens of articles about the antioxidants, polyphenols, and other healthful enzymes in colourful (red, orange, yellow) fruits and vegetables. Believe it or not, the dark brown coffee bean has similar properties.

In fact, on a global basis, coffee delivers more antioxidants than any other food group, according to the *Journal of Nutrition*. Coffee's health-enhancing qualities probably come from this high delivery of antioxidants. Tea is likewise a potent source of antioxidants and polyphenols, particularly green tea. While most endurance performance studies have used coffee as the primary stimulant, tea delivers similar, albeit less-pronounced, benefits.

**Boost your endurance:** Many runners prize coffee for the way it gets them up and moving on early-morning runs. Of course, it can do the same in the late afternoon. None of us wants to start any workout feeling fatigued. Coffee can reverse that, and possibly improve several health markers at the same time.

In mid-2016, the *International Journal of Sports Nutrition and Exercise Metabolism* published a review of more than 600 coffee and performance experiments. The journal concluded that pre-event coffee consumption improved completion times by 3.1 percent – a very large difference in scientific terms.

That said, race-day mornings will require careful planning. A cup or two of coffee can help you run faster, but may also necessitate paying more attention to bathroom visits. Be sure to use coffee on training runs to know how your system will react. Try caffeine tabs – one 200 mg tab should do fine – if you need an alternative.

# 8

# Probiotics

I ADMIT IT: I'm a little ahead of the curve on this one. We've all read miracle claims about probiotics and the importance of a healthy, thriving microbiome. But they haven't been around long enough for Western scientists to complete multi-year studies.

In this case, I'm a fan based on a rather dramatic personal injury and disease I suffered in the winter of 2013/2014. I got so sick I doubted I could start the 2014 Boston Marathon – the race everyone wanted to enter twelve months after the Boston bomb explosions and deaths. We wanted to show our resilience. Me? I could barely get off the sofa for four months.

This episode began with an easy 8-mile trail run through a scenic coastal preserve. My foot caught on something, and I pitched forward, hitting the ground hard. When I scrambled to my feet, I was bleeding from the knees, hip, and elbows, particularly on my right side. It took some effort to walk and jog the 2 miles back to my car.

At home, my wife helped me clean up, but then insisted I visit a nearby medical clinic. The doc gave me two strong antibiotics to fight off possible infections. Several days later, I started to experience terrible diarrhoea. It just wouldn't let up. In two weeks, I lost fifteen pounds from my already thin frame. Day by day, I felt more listless.

Next I fell into major clinical depression. Yes, I saw a couple of psychiatrists, who didn't help much. Most days I got no farther from my bed than the living-room sofa. I sat there for hours on end, too consumed by dark broodings to read or even watch TV. I won't say I had suicidal plans, but I definitely concluded that life wasn't worth living in this manner.

A lab test revealed that I had a microbiome disease called 'c diff' for clostridium difficile. The route to recovery was uncertain. My family attended to my every need, and my closest friends called daily. Nothing helped.

Eventually, after four months, my body just turned. It began edging back towards equilibrium. One day I actually felt like running a mile. The next day wasn't too bad either. I seized on the momentum, and did everything I could to keep it going.

Three months later I completed the 2014 Boston Marathon in the slowest time of my life. Happy? You'd better believe it.

As I recovered, I read more about the microbiome and its connection to everything from the immune system to the brain. I resolved to keep mine as healthy as possible through diet and probiotic supplements. I also learned that antibiotics can deplete the microbiome. Be careful with them.

**Eat plain yogurt with your favourite yummies:** Yogurt is pretty much the original probiotic food, available in a vast variety of textures and flavours. Buy plain yogurt to avoid the excessive sugar in many prepared yogurts, and mix in a variety of your favourite fixings. I add sunflower seeds, wheatgerm, walnuts, bananas, strawberries, and blueberries, often with a touch of honey or maple syrup. Scrumptious!

Once introduced to Greek yogurt a few years back, I jumped on board. I love the thick consistency of Greek yogurt, plus the extra protein. Special bonus: A 2016 'systematic review' of yogurt studies found that it 'is associated with lower body mass index, lower body weight/weight gain, smaller waist circumference and lower body fat'.

**Use kefir to make smoothies:** Probiotic foods are ones that have gone through a fermentation process. Kefir is like a liquid yogurt, but contains even more healthful bacteria than yogurt. I use it in smoothies with a banana and several heaping tablespoons of vanilla whey protein (and sometimes even peanut butter). These smoothies are thick, tasty, protein-packed, and filling. They have replaced the ice-cream-based milkshakes that I craved and often drank fifty years ago.

**Add kimchi or sauerkraut to your salads:** I first encountered kimchi – a spicy, pickled cabbage – while attending the 1988 Olympics in Seoul, South Korea. I didn't go back for a second helping. I've since learned to add a small amount to the salads I eat almost every evening. As with other probiotics, it doesn't take much to have a positive effect.

# 9

# Running and Weight Loss

MANY RUNNERS TAKE up the sport to lose weight. It's no wonder, given that 70 percent of Americans are overweight or obese these days, while runners mostly occupy the other end of the spectrum. It seems clear that running should lead to weight loss.

And it often does. The stories of people who have taken up running and dropped 50 pounds, 100 pounds, even 150 pounds are legion. You could become one of them. But these are just stories – random anecdotes. When researchers explore the connection between exercise and weight loss, they almost always find a more nuanced picture.

First and most important, running will make you fitter and healthier even if you don't reach your fantasy weight goal. Literally thousands of studies have proven this. Running and other consistent aerobic exercise lowers the risk of heart disease, diabetes, cancer, and high blood pressure – the major so-called 'lifestyle diseases'. No wonder health experts argue that fitness is more important than fatness.

Second, running and walking are the best ways to keep off any pounds you lose. That's a big deal, because short-term weight loss is relatively easy, but long-term weight loss maintenance is very difficult. Few achieve it.

Many who do succeed have shared their secrets with the National Weight Control Registry. Among their habits: eating breakfast, weighing themselves often, and walking or running an hour a day. Exercise keeps the pounds off.

But calorie cutting is more effective at producing the initial weight loss, according to most experts. They don't care what diet you choose, so long as it's one you can maintain for the rest of your life. Nutrition experts also endorse regular aerobic exercise for its many health benefits.

The two-pronged approach is one we can all agree upon. The best diet and exercise programmes are the ones you can sustain not just for three months, or maybe six. But for the rest of your days. Optimal health must be a lifelong pursuit.

**Eliminate sugary drinks:** Runners tend to hydrate a lot, and too many of their favourite drinks include too much sugar. Even fruit juices are loaded with sugar, albeit natural sugars. Substitute water for all calorie-laden drinks. It's the easiest way to reduce your daily calorie intake, and lose weight, while ensuring that you also hydrate sufficiently.

**Cut sweet, fatty foods like cakes and cookies:** Every gram of fat adds nine calories to your total daily count versus just four calories each for carbs and protein. In addition, fats are less filling than the other two groups, and require fewer calories to assimilate fully. This digestive process, called the thermic effect of food, can 'erase' as much as 30 percent of the proteins you eat, and 20 percent of the carbohydrates, but only 5 percent of fats.

Cut out all the sweet, fatty foods you can. No one achieves perfection in this department. We all enjoy a tasty-but-sinful treat on occasion, and that's okay. Just keep these occasions to a minimum.

**Aim for volume, not density:** One of the most proven weight-loss methods is to increase the volume of your food while decreasing the calorie density. This system even has a name, Volumetrics. It was first pointed out by University of Pennsylvania nutrition researcher, Barbara Rolls, PhD.

Salads are low-calorie but high-volume because lettuce and vegetables contain a lot of water and fibre. Add a little protein to the top of your salad – such as fish or chicken – and it becomes a complete meal. Avoid 'high-energy density' foods such as potato chips, french fries, ice cream, cookies, and the like.

**Skip the burgers and pizza:** Sad to say, but our favourite fast foods are also among the least healthy, and most likely to pack on pounds. Both burgers and pizza are high in salt and saturated fats. Far better to choose alternative meals.

Many pizza fans convince themselves that a little tomato sauce and a few veggie slices are enough to make pizza a healthy food. Unfortunately, that's not the case. Even if you pile on extra veggies, you won't change the basic equation much. Pizza ranks as the fifth most frequently eaten food in the USA, and is hence a major contributor to the obesity crisis.

# 10

# Vitamins and Supplements

RUNNERS ARE UNUSUALLY health-conscious, and therefore tend to take multi-vitamin, mineral, and other supplements to 'ensure' optimal body functioning. There's little to no evidence that this is an effective strategy, but we continue anyway. Fans believe they are paying a small price for extra protection. Sceptics claim the pills do nothing but produce expensive urine, since the body eliminates excess amounts.

I'm probably the world's most irregular consumer of vitamins and supplements. Every six months or so I'll decide it's time to return to a basic multi-vitamin pill. I'll rush out to the store, buy a fresh supply of thick, grainy pills that are virtually impossible to swallow, and take one-a-day for … three or four days.

Of course I won't notice any difference in how I feel. I don't have more energy or run faster or jump higher or any of the other things that I would like to gain from the pills.

So I'll forget them for a couple of days. They'll drift deeper to the back of the refrigerator until they disappear. Out of sight, out of mind. I don't take them for the next six months.

Then I'll read a magazine or newspaper report, and decide that I absolutely need to begin taking Vitamin D, or a beet supplement, or maybe turmeric – a recently popular herb used in Indian curries. I buy the new supplements, take them for a couple of days . . . and then repeat the process I've just reported above.

This is no way for anyone to enact a supplement plan. I'm certainly not recommending it. Mostly, I'm pointing out that runners are always looking for that special advantage, but it's very difficult to find one. I've taken a variety of supplements through the years, and I can't point to one that has made me feel better, or run stronger.

That's not a complete condemnation. I keep expecting that eventually I'll find something that works. However, when researchers have studied the benefits of vitamins and other supplements, the results have been notably mixed. A 2014 report from the US Preventive Services Task Force concluded that 'the current evidence is insufficient to assess the benefits and harms of multivitamins for the prevention of cardiovascular disease or cancer'. It further recommended against the use of beta-carotene or Vitamin E supplements.

**Eat foods, not pills:** While studies of multi-vitamin pills often produce confounding and conflicting results, reports on the foods that contain the most vitamins and minerals (ie, fruit and vegetables), always seem to yield positive findings. A 2017 meta-analysis of fruit and vegetable consumption in the *International Journal of Epidemiology* concluded: 'Fruit and vegetable intakes were associated with reduced risk of cardiovascular disease, cancer, and all-cause mortality.'

**Fish oil benefits:** The World Health Organization recommends that everyone eat several servings of fish a week, but not everyone enjoys fish. That's one big reason why fish oil capsules containing ample amounts of omega-3 fatty acids are among the most popular of supplements. These pills also have a long list of potential benefits, including better mental health, reduced heart disease, and lower levels of inflammation. Be cautious if you are at risk for prostate cancer, since a 2016 report showed a link between fish oil and increased risk of prostate cancer.

**Consider glucosamine or chondroitin:** Several decades ago, a *Runner's World* survey revealed that more than 80 percent of readers were taking glucosamine and/or chondroitin supplements to prevent knee pain and injury. Since the supplements had no major side effects, taking them seemed an easy and risk-free decision. Runners will do just about anything to avoid knee pain.

The popularity of glucosamine and chondroitin suffered little after a double-blind, placebo-controlled experiment released in 2010 found no evidence to support the supplements.

On the other hand, a 2017 study in *Annals of Rheumatic Diseases* concluded that 800 mg a day of 'pharmaceutical grade chondroitin sulphate' relieved knee pain better than the prescription drug Celebrex.

# 11

# The Vegetarian or Vegan Way

AN UNEXPECTEDLY HIGH percentage of runners are vegetarians, or even vegans, though no one knows why for certain. It could be that some runners believe vegetarian diets are healthy (they are!), or a path to faster performances. Others might choose to lose weight or stay lean the vegetarian way, another proven effect.

Runners also tend to support clean air, clean water, and healthy soil, which are often related to vegetarian practices. Still others oppose the killing of other sentient animals.

I was drawn to vegetarianism at age seventeen by many of the above factors, but mainly through the influence of my coach and mentor, John J. Kelley. Minutes after we finished long, sweltering summer runs, Kelley would grab his shovel and dig into his backyard compost pile and garden.

At first, as a new convert to cross-country running, I mainly wanted to get faster. I supposed that almost any exotic foods might help – yogurt, wheatgerm oil, avoiding meat. When General Mills introduced a new whole-wheat cereal named 'Total', I was instantly hooked.

I couldn't resist a food claiming to contain 100 percent of many vitamins and minerals. While others in my high school wolfed down pizza and burgers for lunch, I munched a container of dry Total with no milk, sugar, or other toppings. You won't be surprised that no one ever asked to swap lunch foods with me.

In those early years, I knew little about the nutrition side of vegetarianism. Looking back I'm amazed that I survived. In fact, I ran my fastest times and won my biggest races, including the Boston Marathon, in those days. I'm sure my heavy training and laser-like motivation were bigger factors than my diet.

Still, the diet worked, and soon there were many magazines, books, and ultimately websites where I could learn more about vegetarianism. I've been well satisfied with my results and my personal health. I've also met a handful of other accomplished endurance athletes who thrived on vegan and vegetarian diets.

Understand your Vitamin B-12 needs: A Vitamin B-12 deficiency can be a problem for vegetarians, since liver and other meats are the best sources. Yet I was not aware of a concern until I hit sixty. Suddenly I felt that I was more fatigued than I should be. From a laboratory blood test, I learned that I had grown deficient in Vitamin B-12, so I began getting monthly shots. Problem solved. A few years later, I switched to B-12 pills (2000 mg/day), and the good results continued.

**Don't sweat the protein:** When I first switched to a vegetarian diet as a teenager, everyone warned that I would fail to get enough protein. The early books were full of exacting instructions on how to eat beans, corn, and other 'complementary proteins' in the same meal to ensure maximum protein availability. Now we know that a narrow time window is not critical. If you consume a variety of protein foods across the day, you'll do fine.

Of course, eggs and dairy products are excellent protein foods as well. In particular, modern nutrition has shown that regular egg consumption is not dangerous to the heart. I enjoy an ample vegetable omelette several times a week.

**Ward off anaemia:** Vegetarian diets are often poor in heme iron, the most biologically active form of iron, found mainly in meats. While many vegetarian foods contain iron, it often isn't readily available to the body tissues. One good trick: Cook with a cast iron pan. Some of the iron will scrape off into your foods. Or combine foods rich in Vitamin C – like fruits, for example – with iron-containing foods like soybeans, tofu, and fortified breakfast cereals. If necessary, use ferrous sulphate supplements.

Consume enough calories to support your running: Some vegetarian runners are such fastidious eaters that they don't consume enough calories on a daily basis. This can spiral downward if you're not careful. It could lead to illness and/or injury.

Try not to be overly restrictive about what you eat. Far better to consume a wide variety of foods, including some high-calorie foods like the healthy fats in nuts, olive oil, avocadoes, and dark chocolate. Food is meant to sustain us, and be enjoyable. Even vegan and vegetarian runners can eat many different foods.

## 12

# The Super-Salad Solution

I ENJOY ASKING friends to come over for dinner, but they don't always appreciate the invite. Many are sceptical of my cooking. That's because they've seen and heard that I don't follow directions. I mean, I can't. I'm just genetically incapable of reading and following all the small-print instructions.

I much prefer kitchen creativity. I like to invent dishes no one has ever concocted before. These often include unusual ingredients that I mix together in novel ways. Unfortunately, 'unusual' and 'novel' don't rank high on the list of adjectives most people apply to their favourite meals.

I'll admit it: Some of my concoctions don't come out as well as I would like. I seem to have a particular problem with pancakes and waffles. Mine usually have the consistency of soggy newspaper. And my bean casseroles too often taste like cheap, over-spiced Mexican food. I guess I should be more careful about hot-pepper flakes and Tabasco sauce.

Surprisingly, I do have a speciality that actually meets with widespread approval. When I prepare my humongous dinner salads for groups of runners and other friends, I get many admiring comments. 'This is really good.' Then I hear the familiar question: 'What did you put into this salad?'

I always respond the same way: 'Everything but the kitchen sink.' Which is pretty much accurate.

My salads are expansive and colourful. I reach for the sky. No limits. If there's something fresh and zesty in the kitchen that I can slice and dice, I go for it. Moments later, it gets tossed into my cavernous salad bowl to make friends with whatever else has preceded it.

Of course, I skimp on the salad dressings. I don't want to ruin a good meal with a commercial dressing, heavy on fats, sugars, and salts. Instead, I opt for extra virgin olive oil and a quality vinegar, perhaps with fresh ground pepper and a salt-free herb-and-vegetable seasoning. Sometimes, I combine olive oil, lemon juice, and honey for a slightly tart, slightly sweet dressing. I like to add a few raisins and a crumble of gorgonzola cheese to top off my salads.

It's a good thing these salads are my supreme creation, for several important reasons. First, I eat a large salad for dinner four to five times a week. Second, it's hard to imagine a dish that's healthier and tastier than an adventurous salad.

**Start with super-green greens:** I've tried just about every possible combination of greens in my salads, but always return to kale, spinach, and rocket. I find all three of these tasty, nutritious, and slightly different in texture. Texture is important to a great salad. It should be sometimes crunchy and sometimes soft, offering the mouth a range of experiences. I like to add purple cabbage for a bold and unexpected tint, in addition to the extra crunch.

**Add as much colour as possible:** This is where I enjoy getting carried away. I include carrots (of course), red, orange, or yellow peppers, and a range of fruit. In my first forty years, I got so tired of salads with lifeless tomatoes that I rarely include them any longer. Instead, I opt for apples, oranges, mangoes, or grapes (of various colours). If I can locate a ripe avocado at the market, it always finds its way into the mix.

**Don't overlook protein:** A salad becomes a truly complete and super-nutritious meal when it includes protein. To this end, I often add tofu and beans (red, black, white – more colours!). Since I eat chicken and fish occasionally, these find a way to the top of my salads from time to time. I'm always thinking about small portions of protein.

**Nuts. Seeds. And more nuts:** I can no longer make any salad without one or several nuts and seeds. My favourites are walnuts, almonds, unsalted sunflower seeds and unsalted peanuts. I use the nuts instead of croutons, which are too fatty and salty. Nuts add healthy, satisfying calories (protein and fat) to the salad, not to mention the wonderful way they increase the texture and crunch factors.

# SECTION 3

# GOING FARTHER

# Unconventional Wisdom

AFTER 10 MILES, I still had a big smile on my face. I felt smooth and comfortable. I had found my rhythm among the more than 15,000 other runners in South Africa's famous Comrades Marathon. Good thing. There were 46 miles left – twenty more than I had ever run before. And I had no inkling that I was about to learn one of the most important lessons of my life in running.

I had been dreaming about getting to Comrades for thirty years, from the first time I read about it in the mid-1960s. No other race could match its history and unique traditions. For one, the course changes direction every year – one year it goes 'up' from Durban to Pietermaritzburg. The next, it goes 'down' from P'burg to Durban. (As with with downhill Boston Marathon, both routes are hilly. Both test one's mental and physical powers.)

The first Comrades took place in 1921 as a tribute to South African World War I veterans. The very name 'comrades' refers to their unyielding support for each other. One South African soldier, Vic Clapham, marched in a sweltering 1,600-mile pursuit of the German forces in East Africa. He organised the annual Comrades to honour his fellow soldiers and their endurance.

In just a few years, Comrades became the most famous sporting event in a sports-mad country. Runners didn't enter to run as fast as they could but rather to finish within the twelve-hour time limit. This earned them a bronze finisher's medal. After collecting ten bronzes, you qualified for a highly-prized green number.

This number didn't just get you an admiring look from other participants. It was yours in perpetuity. Literally. You owned it. No one else would ever be given the same number in the Comrades Marathon. This is, in my mind, the grandest tradition in all of running.

Elite runners might one day win an Olympic gold medal. But merely determined runners could win an absolutely unique Comrades green number for all time. They simply had to put in the sweat, toil, and tears required to finish ten Comrades. This required no special talent, but a world of endurance.

Given that I had to fly 8,000 miles to reach the 1994 Comrades start line, I knew I would never earn a green number. But I wanted that bronze finisher's medal. And things were going very well.

Until I hit the first hill at 10 miles on the way to Umlaas Road. Suddenly I faced a total gridlock of bodies in front of me. Everyone had stopped running. They were all walking. I wanted none of this. I was a proud Boston Marathon winner. I had travelled to South Africa to run Comrades, not to walk it.

I darted to my right, and squeezed through an opening. I zigged left to find another, then zagged back to the right, turned sideways to make myself as thin as possible, and gently pushed myself forward between two big-chested runners. In a matter of minutes, I passed several hundred, but the effort was stupid.

I still had 46 miles to go. Minutes before, I had been flowing along almost effortlessly. Now I felt myself huffing and puffing, as if I were running frenzied intervals. Everyone else was strolling along happy as could be. I asked myself: What's wrong with this picture?

Fortunately, I came to my senses. The walkers all around me knew exactly what they were doing. They had finished many previous Comrades – and many wore a green number to prove it – with the simple strategy of walking the steepest uphills to save their legs and lungs for the flats and downhills. There were a lot of miles to come, and it was more important to conserve oneself for the last half-dozen of those miles than to scurry uphill now.

The Comrades runners were geniuses. And I – the first-timer – was an idiot not to have comprehended their method. I let my hubris get in the way of clear thinking.

I jammed on the brakes, and joined the happy throng walking to the top of Umlaas Road. When my comrades started running again, I followed suit. When they walked at the next significant hill, I did the same. It was blissful.

The internet hadn't reached its full flowering by 1994, and I didn't yet know the term 'crowd sourcing', which I also refer to as 'collective wisdom'. But I experienced it full-force at the 10-mile mark of that year's Comrades Marathon. The crowd around me – a large group with many years of experience – knew exactly what they were doing.

I had some credentials, too. I was a Boston Marathon winner, after all, and could probably run a faster 26-mile race than most of the Comrades crew. I was the editor of *Runner's World*, which meant I had access to advice from famous runners, coaches, and sports scientists. I had read many magazine articles and several books about Comrades, so I was well versed in the race history.

Yet I knew almost nothing about how to actually run the 56 miles between P'burg and Durban. I was a complete rookie. The crowd around me all held PhDs. They had earned their advanced degrees the hard way – by trial-and-error experimentation through a handful, a dozen, or even several dozen prior Comrades. These weren't quitters. They were students, and finishers.

Collective wisdom plays an important role in many other areas of running, and I've included the best examples in *Run Forever*. There's no mathematical proof to the Ten Percent Rule. It's just a great rule-of-thumb.

Similarly, no one knows for certain that beginners should follow the walk-run method, or that marathoners need to cover 20 miles in training. But these tried-and-true techniques have worked in countless cases. We should never disregard the collective wisdom. It's a great and handy guide.

One thing I'm sure of: I never ran smarter than the day I followed the collective wisdom of thousands of Comrades runners. Once I saw what they were doing, and how, I stuck with them all the way. My Boston Marathon winner's medal could do me no good on the road to Durban. My South African comrades showed the way.

They got me to the finish line inside the Durban Cricket Stadium more than an hour ahead of the cut-off time. And I've got the Vic Clapham bronze medal to prove it.

## 1

# The Ten Percent Rule

RUNNERS FREQUENTLY GET injured from running too much and/or increasing their weekly mileage too fast. To avoid such training errors, you need a plan – a plan you will stick to. I could put it to you colloquially: Be careful, very careful. Be gradual, very gradual.

But there's actually a time-honoured numerical rule for building your mileage. It's the Ten Percent Rule. You should follow it closely.

The Ten Percent Rule states: Increase your weekly training mileage by no more than ten percent per week. If you run 10 miles this week, you should run no more than 11 miles next week, and 12 miles the week after. If you start at 20 miles a week, you can run 22 and 24 miles in the next two weeks. And so on.

The rule strikes many – especially young, achievement-hungry runners – as very conservative. That's exactly the point. A gradual, step-by-step increase in your weekly mileage is calculated to give your joints, muscles, and tendons time to adapt. They will get stronger, not overwhelmed. You will gain efficiency and endurance while minimising the risk of injury.

At the same time, you'll roughly double your mileage in a ten-week period. That's a very impressive gain. Millions have used the Ten Percent Rule to go from couch-to-5K in just a couple of months. Ditto for an amazing number of first-time marathoners. You can be conservative, and still accomplish bold goals.

Better to be safe than sorry. Better to keep moving forward than to be sitting injured on the sidelines ... and moving backward. Slow-but-sure is almost always the best path to follow in your training, your nutrition, and your racing.

Remember: Lifetime running amounts to a Turtle versus Hare competition. In this showdown, the most important one you'll face in running, the Turtle always wins. Always.

**Don't run more days:** To increase your weekly mileage, you could of course add another day to your training schedule. If you're currently running on Monday, Wednesday, and Friday, for example, you could add Saturday. This would give you a nice boost in mileage, but wouldn't be a smart approach.

Whenever you add to your running load, the body needs extra recovery. Another day of running can only reduce that recovery. Don't ask for trouble. Better to go a mile or two longer on your existing workout days, and to keep giving your body the recovery days it has grown accustomed to.

**An alternative rule:** If you don't have enough patience to follow the Ten Percent Rule, there's an alternative that still has a built-in 'governor'. This one is called the Repeat It Rule, and some great coaches and runners swear by it. The Repeat It Rule states: Always run at least two weeks in a row at the same mileage before bumping up to the next level.

In other words, you can start at 12 miles and increase to 15 – please don't get too greedy about the increases – but then you must repeat the 15-mile week before moving upward again. Your progression might look like: 12, 12, 15, 15, 18, 18, and so on. Again, this system is designed to give your body time to accept and adapt to heavier training loads.

**Keep all runs slow and relaxed:** As a general principle, you should never attempt to build mileage and speed at the same time. First, mileage. Later, speed. That means, when increasing mileage, you should do all your runs at a slow, relaxed pace.

This principle would be easy to violate. As you run more, you often become more efficient, which means you can also run faster. Avoid the temptation. If necessary, even reduce your effort to keep your pace at the same relaxed level.

Here's a personal trick: I like to meditate before running. I simply sit in a chair, and breathe slowly and deeply for several minutes. It always makes my runs feel fresher and less frantic. I don't push the envelope, edging into a faster pace every mile. Instead, I find I can maintain my calm throughout the run.

## 2

# Training Partners

RUNNING EXPERTS DON'T always agree on the most productive ways to train, but they are nearly unanimous when it comes to one subject: The best stimulus to more and better running is a good training partner.

This principle has stood the test of time, and proved incredibly useful to every kind of runner. Olympians gather together in training camps or sponsored groups to motivate and push each other to new heights. Meanwhile, in neighbourhoods and parks across the world, recreational runners gather for encouragement and improvement.

Here's an example. On a Sunday morning in 1969, a handful of runners met up in Palos Verdes, California, for an easy 6 miles. They enjoyed it so much that they decided to do the same thing again the following Sunday. Almost fifty years later, the 'Breakfast Club' is still going strong.

Some of the original group continue to run a slow 6 miles. Others show up for the social time, and to walk 3 miles before breakfast. The weekly turnout reached fifty or more runners in the mid-1980s; now it's about half that size. But it still takes place every Sunday morning. You can count on it. That's the great thing about training partners.

In 2017, one of the original Breakfast Club members published a medical article about fifty-four of his running buddies. Remarkably enough, Ben Rosin, a cardiologist, found that his training partners were living nineteen years longer, on average, than equivalent, non-running males. 'My data show that marathon runners have a low rate of cardiovascular disease, and great longevity,' Rosin told me. 'High intensity, high endurance running appears to have significant benefits.'

Increased longevity is certainly a good reason to search out a running partner or training group. And there are many more. Social running is fun, and it keeps you honest. It's too easy to ignore your own best intentions. It's much harder to stand up a friend. Training partners offer exactly the help you need to run more and farther.

**Look for pace compatibility:** You can find potential training partners through local running stores or clubs, as well as social media. Just make sure you team up with someone who runs at roughly the same pace as you. The sex and age of your training partners doesn't matter. But their fitness and ability do.

Don't run regularly with someone who's faster than you are. That leads down the road to injury and burnout. It's also annoying to both parties if one of you is always looking over a shoulder and slowing for the other. No one likes that situation, whether you're the one up front or the one behind.

**A word about politics and personality:** You're not going to marry your training partner. (Well, this has certainly happened, but it's not the norm.) So you don't need to match up perfectly on a wide range of topics and philosophies. That said, the more you agree in key areas, the better your running relationship will be.

My favourite training partners have included Mad Dog and The Engineer. Mad Dog is short, Irish, and pugnacious. He got me into a few nervous situations, particularly when he gave his best regards to motorists who had likewise saluted us on the roadways. But Mad Dog was fun, reliable, very hard working, and pace compatible. What more could I ask for?

The Engineer is totally different, and much the same. He taught me things about mechanical engineering I would never have learned on my own. Best of all, being an engineer, he ran at a constant, metronomic pace perfectly suited to mine. We spent a delightful decade spurring each other to top efforts.

**Save several runs for yourself:** While running with partners is wonderful, it's also good to save workout days for yourself. These could be your easy days or your hard days. It depends on your own training plan and race goals, as well as your partner's.

I've always enjoyed running with people – old friends and new acquaintances – but I also like to run by myself. On solo days, I can completely control the time of the workout, the pace, the location, my meals before and after, and more. This has great appeal, especially on busy days when I don't have time to meet a training partner at some location other than my front door.

# 3

# Cut-Back Weeks

THE GOAL OF all mileage-building programmes is to reach a certain level on a specific date. You might simply want to increase your training base. More likely, you are aiming for an upcoming race like a half-marathon or marathon. Either way, the path is rarely straight and flat. Everyone encounters obstacles. The question is: Can you train smart enough to avoid most of the pitfalls?

Early in my marathon career, I had trouble with this. I noticed a disturbing trend. After circling my race date on a calendar, I'd count back sixteen weeks, and devise my training plan. It looked foolproof on paper, but rarely worked out that way. Time and again, I'd get sick or injured about two-thirds to three-quarters of the way through the programme.

At first, I couldn't figure out what was wrong. After all, I was following the rule of gradual progression in training. Nothing in my plan looked blatantly stupid. The slope of my weekly miles inched upward at a modest rate.

After several years of unsatisfactory marathon results, I decided to create a different kind of plan. My weekly training mileage didn't fit a straight line. Instead, once a month, it dipped. During that week, I decreased my mileage instead of continuing the gradual increase. I called this a 'cut-back week'.

I stopped short at the weekly long run, however. I figured the long run was so important I needed to do one every week, always a little longer than the previous one. So my cut-back week was six days. I was afraid to extend it to seven days.

My new plan proved better than my old way, but I still wasn't satisfied with the results. So I tried again. This time, I cut back my long runs once a month as well. Now my cut-back week was a full seven days long, meaning that once a month I had 13 days of recovery between long runs.

The new approach worked great. After a full cut-back week, I felt energised to begin the next month of marathon training. I didn't get sick or injured as frequently as in the past. Soon I began telling my friends about cut-back weeks, and writing about them in *Runner's World*. I said that full cut-back weeks especially helped runners deal with the 'monster month' of marathon training just before the taper period (see pages 190-192).

Building mileage and preparing for marathons aren't easy. I would never claim that they are. But they are much more manageable when your plan includes regular cut-back weeks.

**Once a month, run 40 to 50 percent less:** Let's say you're up to 16 miles a week after three weeks of your marathon training plan. Don't increase to 18 or 20 miles on week four. Instead, drop back to 8 to 12 miles. After this recovery week, you can jump up to 18 to 20 miles in week five.

Repeat the same pattern during weeks eight and twelve. By then you may be running twice as much as you were at the outset of your training. As your weekly mileage gets higher, the cut-back weeks become even more important. They give both mind and body the recharge period necessary to keep going. Don't ever underestimate the mental part.

**Apply the same rule to your weekly long run:** All marathon training programmes focus on increasing the distance of your long run. This approach makes complete sense. Elite runners also need to consider their pace. Others don't. For 99 percent of marathon runners, the key ingredient is to build up time on the road.

In some programmes, you run just twice a week: a long run and an easy run. Other plans are more ambitious. Whichever you choose, I suggest you reduce the distance of your long run on weeks four, eight, and twelve. A 40 percent cut-back works well. The final cut-back on week twelve will leave you just one or two more long runs before you begin to taper. That's perfect.

**Try other cut-back methods:** While I've proposed that you cut back on your fourth, eighth, and twelfth weeks, the numbers aren't special. It's simply a system that fits neatly into a sixteen-week training plan. Feel free to experiment with other cut-back plans – every sixth week, for example, or every third week, or even every other week. The only essential is that you give yourself a necessary recovery period when you need it most.

# 4

# Run-Walk for Distance

I CAME LATE to a full appreciation for run-walk training and racing. When I was young, I had no need for walking breaks. I just tried to go farther and faster on my runs. By the time I reached my mid-fifties, however, I could see that it was time for a change. I grew more interested in lifetime running than in running fast today. That's when I began experimenting seriously with run-walk, and learning how useful and flexible it could be.

Strangely enough, back in the 1960s, I was college roommates with Jeff Galloway, the author-runner-coach who has popularised run-walk. We never talked about it back then. Instead we did workouts like 40 x 400 metres with a 50-meter jog. Jeff was the hardest, most consistent trainer I had ever met. It didn't surprise me when he made the US Olympic team in 1972.

In truth, Jeff wasn't the inspiration for my first run-walk effort. That came from Tom Osler, a top 1960s marathoner who enjoyed historical research into distance running. Osler proposed that 15 minutes of running, followed by five of walking, was the ideal ratio to cover prodigious distances. One day in the early 1970s, I actually ran 50 miles this way. I felt fresh the whole way. The next day, I wasn't even sore.

But I wasn't about to become an ultra-marathoner at that time, so I didn't do another run-walk until I reached my mid-fifties, when I began leading *Runner's World* marathon pace teams at major marathons around the country. I always led the 3:59 group. We did 9 minutes of running, followed by a 1-minute walk break, and always finished a minute or two under our 4 hour goal time.

A decade later, in private efforts in the Boston Marathon, I switched to 4 minutes of running, and 1 of walking. I finished five straight Bostons – and counting – with times that ranged from 4:15 to 4:30. That's the best part of run-walk. You can tailor it to your personal needs and goals. I expect to be experimenting with different ratios for the rest of my running life. And I'm looking forward to every mile of it.

**Run less, go longer:** All runners aiming to increase their endurance must gradually cover longer and longer distances. Coaches and athletes often speak of 'time on the feet', another way of saying the same thing. This becomes particularly important when you are training for a marathon.

A run-walk strategy offers the best, most proven method to increase time on your feet. For example, if you've been running for 30 minutes at a time, you might want to increase to 60. You could get there in a month or so by increasing the time of your longest run by 5 to 10 minutes per week.

But there's an easier, more immediate way. Simply switch from running to a run-walk routine. For example, run 2 minutes, walk 1, and repeat. You could probably hit 60 minutes tomorrow. You'll gain confidence, and learn a lot about the power of run-walk.

**Run more, walk less:** As you get fitter and stronger, you'll want to adjust your run-walk ratio. You'll want to bump up the running, and decrease the walking. This is only natural, and there's nothing wrong with it. Just be careful not to overdo it.

Let's say you've been using a 2-1 pattern – 2 minutes of running, 1 of walking. You've reached two hours of time on your feet. What next? You could just keep going longer, of course. Or you could switch to a 3-1 pattern for your two-hour training effort. This should be doable, and it will also increase your fitness, since it's harder than 2-1.

As you gain fitness this way, you will run farther and faster, no matter what run-walk ratio you choose. You put yourself into a positive cycle of success.

**Vary your ratios:** Clearly, run-walk is a great way for first-time marathoners to train for and race the distance. Tens of thousands have followed this path, settling into their own preferred run-walk ratio. Jeff Galloway himself now covers marathons with a ratio of 15 seconds of running, and 15 seconds of walking. This sounds almost ludicrous, but Jeff does it once a month, often with his wife, Barbara. He swears that it produces the best marathon-recovery ever.

One thing I know for sure about run-walk. If you allow yourself to accept it, run-walk will open more doors than you can possibly imagine. It is the most important tool for lifetime running, from your earliest, perhaps youthful days on the tracks and roads, to the continued healthy running of your later years. Give it a try.

# 5

# Long Runs

THE LONG RUN is so crucial to a runner's endurance goals that you've got to find a way to make it go right. Treat it like a trifle, and you'll encounter unexpected suffering – both mental and physical. Treat it like a special event, on the other hand, and it will likely go much smoother.

Many runners, myself included, develop a ritual around their long runs. For example, I always organise my apparel the night before a long run, just as I do before a race. Whether I'm joining a group the next morning, or going solo, I sleep better knowing that I won't have to wake up and rummage around for my gear.

Far better to be fully prepared for your run. And for other important early-morning preparations. Like a cup of coffee, a slice of toast and jam, or whatever your needs might be.

I also check the weather forecast. It's important to know the expected weather for longer-than-normal workouts. Indeed, nothing else will affect you as much as the weather, and the way you prepare for it. I want to know about temperature, humidity, precipitation, and wind speed and direction.

True, I can't change the weather. But I can make many personal adjustments. For example, I can change my start time by an hour or two, seek a course where I will have plenty of hydration options, or switch to a somewhat-sheltered route if I'm concerned about high winds. Every veteran runner makes many small-but-effective changes for long runs.

**Here's one of mine:** I like to have something to pop in my mouth during long runs. For many years now, a simple drugstore peppermint candy has been my favourite. I don't kid myself about an energy boost. I doubt the candy contains more than a dozen calories. I simply find it pleasant and refreshing to let a mint dissolve in my mouth while I'm running.

If I'm going really long, say more than 15 miles, I might carry a commercial energy gel or bloc with caffeine. I don't honestly get a major caffeine buzz from these things. But I've read so many studies with titles like 'Caffeine extends endurance' that I've become a believer. Whether mental or physical, I feel a modest lift after taking a caffeine shot.

**Special meals for special runs:** The carbo-loading pasta party has become such a big part of the long run/marathon tradition that I don't feel right without spaghetti. On other nights before other runs, I don't think much about my dinner meal. But I've been carbo-loading for fifty years before long runs, and can't imagine changing habits now.

Of course, you can eat other carbohydrate-rich foods. It doesn't have to be pasta. Let variety and your taste buds be your guide. Don't let carb hysteria dissuade you. If there's a time for sugar and processed carbs, it's the night before your long runs. The next day, you can return to whole-grain foods.

**Call in your buddies:** Your weeks are probably so busy that you have little time to run with friends. Weekends are different, and long runs typically bring training partners and training groups together to support one another. Get in touch with others, and join or organise a group run. Almost nothing else will make your long run go better.

There's no rule that says everyone has to go the full long-run distance – 16 miles, or whatever it might be. You can join a group that's going a lesser distance, and simply add miles before or after. Every mile with a group adds a little ease to your run. Or arrange for a training partner to meet you after the first hour. There's nothing like a pick-me-up for the final 10 miles.

**Pick a special location:** Chances are, you run similar routes during the week, from home, work, YMCA, or wherever. You don't have a lot of time, and certainly can't afford to waste it. That's one reason I've always run from home or work. Another: I hate the idea of getting into my private car, and driving to my workout location. I'd rather preserve the environment while also minimising wasted time.

That said, I relax these rules for weekend long runs. They are special, and I want to reward myself for doing them. I can't imagine a better way to do this than running with friends in a not-everyday location. So I'll swallow a little eco-pride, and drive to the park, trail, or long and scenic road. Whenever possible, I car pool.

# 6

# Long Run Hydration

NO AREA OF running has received more scientific exploration than the runner's fluid needs. Literally hundreds of studies have investigated what levels of hydration will optimise your health and performance, and how dehydration can do the opposite.

Fifty years ago, health experts knew almost nothing about a runner's fluid needs. Most road races started at noon, because that was when the Boston Marathon started. Race directors of events on July 4 didn't seem to understand the differences between mid-April weather and July conditions. Not only that, but they never considered setting up water tables en route, and no one had ever heard of Gatorade.

Somehow we runners of that era survived. Three decades later, amazingly, the sport had changed so much that runners were more likely to be drinking too much water rather than too little. Sports drink companies were encouraging runners to drink as much as possible. At least, that was the message many marathoners seemed to get.

Then we learned a strange new term for the first time – hyponatraemia, or too little sodium in the blood. This was caused by too much fluid consumption. It turned out that excessive consumption of water and sports drinks wasn't a good thing. Less was more. Hyponatraemia caused a number of deaths to participants in endurance events.

More recently, researchers, sports drink companies, and medical directors at major marathons have settled on a saner approach to hydration. Yes, runners should drink before and during marathon races and long training runs. But the drinking should be moderate.

A small dehydration – about two percent of your body weight – is no cause for alarm. In fact, it's a normal and natural response to several hours of exercise. If you happen to weigh 150 pounds, a two-percent dehydration represents 48 ounces (1.36 litres) that you *do not have to drink* while running.

You can gauge your level of hydration/dehydration without a bathroom scale. Simply check your urine colour. If it's clear or has a straw-like tint, you're fine. If it's a darker yellow, you need to drink. Note: A darker colour is normal in the morning when you've had little or nothing to drink for eight hours.

**Train your gut:** Many runners feel a distressed and nauseous stomach when they consume too much fluid, especially in races. However, the same runners fail to realise that they can train the gut in much the same way they train the leg muscles – little by little.

Begin by drinking slightly more than your usual amount before a workout. If that goes well, try the same procedure again, or increase a bit more. Similarly, drink somewhat more while you are running. Start this process at the onset of warm weather to prepare yourself for what's coming. A stomach that can comfortably hold more fluid will deliver more to the bloodstream, staving off dehydration.

**How much to drink:** Experts at the American College of Sports Medicine recommend that you drink three to six ounces (85 to 170ml)every 20 minutes while running. The range is wide because your body size, your pace, the weather, and your genetics have a large impact. For more precision, you can conduct a simple experiment to determine your personal hydration needs.

Weigh yourself before and after a workout of measured time or distance. Be sure you are naked and dry for both weigh-ins. The weight you lose comes 95 percent from water, not from fat or muscle, so it can be considered your sweat rate. Adjust this loss to either ounces per hour or ounces per mile, whichever you find most useful. Remember that you don't have to replace all your sweat. You simply want to keep the losses to no more than two percent of your body weight.

**Don't confuse dehydration and heatstroke:** Many runners wrongly believe they can avoid heat illness by drinking sufficiently. But heatstroke, the most dangerous form of heat illness and a genuine threat to summer runners, is caused primarily by running too fast for the conditions.

The endurance pace you can tolerate on a hot and humid ninety-degree day is much slower than what you can run on a 50-degree day. If you ignore this basic physiology, you risk a case of heat illness. Some races will cancel when the conditions are too extreme. Others will turn off their timing clocks. You should do the same. You can't beat the heat, not even with extra fluids. Be smart, and run smart.

# 7

# Carbohydrate Loading

EVERYONE GETS IT: To run long, you need fuel. Lots of fuel. That's why we have carbohydrate-loading. It's the best way to make sure your tank is full.

It also explains why I see so many runners on marathon start lines looking as if they are ready for a transcontinental trek. They're wrapped in fuel belts, backpacks, straps, and holsters brimming with every imaginable high-energy food. And quite a few I'd rather not imagine.

However, long-run fuelling doesn't have to be so complex. The human body has a simple, if limited, process by which it stores and then parcels out all the energy needed for long endurance efforts. There are a few key steps you need to get right. Beyond those, you won't gain anything by attempting to haul a spare gas tank along with you.

The body's primary energy source is glycogen – stored glucose (sugar). About 80 percent of your stored glucose is packed in the muscles, and thus readily available when you are running. Since you train on a regular basis, your muscles become quite efficient at storing and utilising this glycogen.

Carbohydrate-loading can also increase your glycogen supply, which explains the popularity of pasta parties the evening before most big marathons. Rice, potatoes, and breads are other simple and excellent sources of carbohydrates.

A little more than 10 percent of your body's glycogen is stored in the liver, which becomes rapidly depleted between meals, and overnight while you sleep. For that reason, nutritionists always advise marathoners to wake up early enough for a modest breakfast. In the long run, every little bit of glycogen helps.

Finally, your bloodstream contains a small amount of circulating glucose. There's not enough glucose to supply much muscle power, but the brain demands carbohydrates around the clock. As I have emphasised at several points in this book: No runner should ever underestimate the importance of a high-functioning brain. Especially in a marathon.

The carbs contained in sports drinks, energy bars, and various gels don't contain enough sugars to do much good. Carry a small supply if you like, but don't overburden yourself (with either excess weight or worry), and don't neglect the more-important, pre-race glycogen basics.

**No need to deplete:** When Scandinavian researchers first explored carbohydrate loading in the late 1960s, they put athletes through a terrible ordeal: a 'depletion' phase before the loading. This meant that marathoners ran a hard 20-miler a week before their event, and followed this fatiguing workout with three days of a low-carb diet. This left their glycogen supply on empty. The marathoners only switched to carb-loading in the final three days before the marathon.

This degree of depletion proved physically and mentally debilitating. Before a marathon, you want to feel strong, eager, and confident. Runners who attempted to deplete felt the opposite: weak, confused, depressed. Yes, they snapped out of it once they began consuming carbs again. But it was a tough road to follow.

Fortunately, researchers eventually discovered an easier way. You don't need to go through the depletion phase. You'll perform just as well – and feel a whole lot better – if you simply reduce your mileage before a marathon while simultaneously switching to high-carb foods for the last two to three days.

**Don't overdo it:** While Frank Shorter was winning the Olympic Marathon in 1972, the American TV audience got its first lesson in carbohydrate loading. The ABC broadcast depicted Shorter's supposed breakfast – a stack of pancakes about two feet high.

I suppose this made the point, but it grossly exaggerated the quantity. To carbohydrate load, you do not have to eat like a starving pig at a trough – not at breakfast, dinner, or any of your meals. In fact, don't eat more than normal. Just reduce fats and proteins (and bulky, high-volume meals like salads), and concentrate on high-carb foods. When in doubt, eat an extra piece of bread or toast.

**The last meal:** Keep it small and simple. Have a bagel, or more of that bread and toast, spread with jam or honey if you have a sweet tooth. Wash it down with water or a favourite sports drink. Many runners find that a banana works well. Some like oatmeal. Don't eat or drink anything that you haven't used many times in the past. Less is more. Eat modestly. Nothing new.

# 8

# Yasso 800s

SOMETIMES THE SIMPLEST training ideas are also the best. Yasso 800s prove this point. A favourite and much-verified marathon workout, Yasso 800s evolved from a happy but random conversation on-the-run.

Several decades ago, I was enjoying a relaxed workout with my *Runner's World* colleague, Bart Yasso. The talk turned to marathon training, as it often does when serious runners get together. We're always trying to figure out new and better ways to prepare for the classic Olympic distance.

On this particular run, Bart began telling me about his personal favourite marathon workout. He would take his goal time for the marathon – let's say 3 hours and 10 minutes – and adapt it to 800 meter repeats by turning the 3 hours and 10 minutes for the marathon into 3 minutes and 10 seconds for each 800 meter repeat. Bart explained that he had discovered he could run a 3:10 marathon when he could do ten 800-meter repeats in 3 minutes and 10 seconds each. Between each of the 800-meter runs, he would walk or jog for the same period of time, three minutes and 10 seconds.

I was startled by Bart's plan. It sounded utterly ridiculous. I had been studying the marathon and marathon training for thirty years, but had never heard of anything remotely similar. Why should the marathon time and 800 time 'line up' so perfectly? It made no sense. I couldn't have been more sceptical.

After finishing the conversation with Bart, I hurried back to my office, and started calling and emailing friends. I asked them all the same two questions: If you did a workout today of ten repeats of 800 metres, what would your average time be? And how fast can you currently run a marathon?

I reached friends who were five-hour marathoners, and one who could run 2:08. And the Yasso formula held true for all of them. It appeared to describe a universal relationship for runners.

The very next day, I sat down and wrote a Yasso 800 training article for *Runner's World*. It first appeared in 2001. Since then, the workout has been successfully validated by tens of thousands of runners around the globe. In her training for the 2017 Boston Marathon, fifty years after her first Boston in 1967, Kathrine Switzer used Yasso 800s to get herself in top shape. 'I walked or jogged really slowly for 3 minutes after each 800, and worked my way up to ten repetitions,' she told me.

Yasso 800s aren't a perfect workout – nothing is – but they come pretty damn close. There's no better way to hone your training for an ambitious marathon time.

**Start with four Yassos:** You can't just go to a track or nearby stretch of road to knock out ten Yasso 800s. As with all other training, you have to build gradually to your goal. I recommend beginning with just four Yasso 800s. This should prove very doable. It's okay to base them on your goal marathon pace, so long as that time is reasonable.

You can also aim for a high-end total of eight Yassos. This is two less than what Bart put himself through, but it's enough to get the job done. And it fits well with my overall training philosophy: A little less is better than too much.

**Add one Yasso a week:** If you're training for a marathon, you've probably selected a twelve- to sixteen-week programme. That's way too many weeks to do Yasso 800s each week. But you can drop the first weeks (of endurance building) and the last weeks (of taper time), leaving room in the middle of your training for Yassos.

Since I believe in starting with four Yassos and increasing to eight, I'd recommend planning five Yasso 800 workouts during your marathon programme. Just stick with the gradual approach, adding one more 800 each time. For example, do four Yasso 800s the first week, five the second, and so on until you reach eight.

**Spread your wings:** While Bart Yasso invented his now-namesake workout specifically for marathon runners, it's a fun and valuable tool for all runners who are trying to improve. The 'numbers' happen to work in a marathon context, but the effort and physiology extend to all race distances.

Basically, the pace of Yasso 800s is a bit slower than optimal interval pace, but somewhat faster than tempo pace. That puts it in the sweet spot of training paces for road runners who typically race distances from the 5K to the half-marathon or marathon.

You can't go wrong running at this intensity. If you're not training for a marathon, there's no need to cram Yasso 800s into a five- to eight-week period. Use them whenever you please, perhaps every two to three weeks, as part of your regular training diet. They're fun, challenging, and numerically precise.

# 9

# Half-Marathon Training

IN RECENT YEARS, the half-marathon has become the second most popular race distance. It has passed the marathon, and moved up on the heels of the 5K. This has been a remarkable development.

Two decades ago, there were almost no half-marathons at all. Most runners raced the 5K, the 10K, and the marathon, occasionally filling in with other distances from 5 miles to 20 kilometres. Then the organisers of the Rock n Roll race series decided to put their marketing might behind the half-marathon distance (13.1 miles). In the process, they created a virtual running revolution.

Now the number of half-marathons have vastly surpassed the marathon-distance races that spawned them. It's easy to understand why. The half-marathon takes much less training than a marathon, and offers a much faster recovery. Most half-marathoners feel like new just a couple of days after the race versus several weeks in the case of those recovering from a full marathon.

Many women and women's groups have been drawn to the half-marathon. It's a challenging distance, but doesn't require the more complete absorption of marathon training. This allows women to lead the balanced lives many aspire to, and has resulted in women making up roughly 60 percent of all participants in US half-marathons.

What's more, the half-marathon has grown into such a major event that there are many exciting travel possibilities. I know one mother-daughter duo who plan to run a half-marathon in each of the fifty states. Last time I checked with them, they had reached the high single-digits, and their enthusiasm seemed to be growing with each race.

Of course, many men and women use the half-marathon as a stepping stone to the marathon. They get a taste of the training and race effort without having to go 'all in'. After one or several half-marathons, you are almost guaranteed success at the 26.2-mile distance. You will know what it takes, and know you're ready for the longer race.

While I applaud the half-marathon's accessibility, I have been mystified by the training approach followed by many. When it comes to the marathon, few would ever think about running beyond 20 miles in training – roughly 80 percent of the race distance. For the half-marathon, on the other hand, many runners seem to feel they must cover the full distance in training before they go to the start line.

This makes no sense since the marathon presents serious glycogen-depletion problems, occurring after about 20 miles, that are not an issue in a half-marathon. If anything, half-marathon training should require shorter long runs, on a percentage basis, than the marathon.

That's why I've created a beginner's half-marathon training programme on pages 120-121 . If you can run 2 miles today, it will get you ready for a half-marathon in just twelve weeks. Like my marathon programme, it's as simple as a plan can be, and yet covers all the training basics.

**Don't sweat the distance:** You don't have to run 13.1 miles in training to complete a half-marathon, just as you don't have to run 26.2 miles for a marathon. If you get up to 8 to 10 miles in training, and run a smart (i.e., conservative, appropriate) pace on race day, you will reach the finish. It only takes race-day determination on top of your solid training efforts.

**Don't obsess about diet and hydration:** They simply are not a big deal when you run a half-marathon. In fact, if you eat and hydrate properly in the twenty-four hours before a half-marathon, you could go the distance without anything more during the race (unless it's unusually hot and humid). That said, who can resist the temptation of multiple aid stations?

Okay, take advantage of the stations. But please don't overdo it. In fact, consider walking at aid tables without actually drinking. Just enjoy the brief respite.

**Run with a buddy:** There's no better way to complete your first half-marathon than to run it with a training partner, or with a pace group provided by the event. I have both led pace teams, and run with pacers at various half-marathons. They always run a steady, even-pace effort that gets you to the finish at the predicted time. It's fun to meet new people at races, and even more fun if one of your regular training partners joins you.

# Beginner's Half-Marathon Training Plan (12 weeks)

THIS PLAN ASSUMES that you can run or run-walk for about 24 minutes (roughly 2 miles) on day one. Your pace stays the same, while your time and distance build slowly and progressively over two weeks.

You will probably find it most convenient to schedule your running for the same three days of every week (for example, Tuesday-Thursday-Saturday), but feel free to adjust.

| Week | Day 1 | | Day 2 | | Day 3 | | Week Totals | |
|---|---|---|---|---|---|---|---|---|
| | Running Time | Approx. Miles | Running Time | Approx. Miles | Running Time | Approx. Miles | Time (hours:minutes) | Miles |
| #1 | 0:24 | 2 | 0:24 | 2 | 0:36 | 3 | 1:24 | 7 |
| #2 | 0:24 | 2 | 0:24 | 2 | 0:48 | 4 | 1:36 | 8 |
| #3 | 0:36 | 3 | 0:36 | 3 | 0:60 | 5 | 2:12 | 11 |
| #4 | 0:36 | 3 | 0:36 | 3 | 1:12 | 6 | 2:24 | 12 |
| #5 | 0:48 | 4 | 0:48 | 4 | 1:24 | 7 | 3:00 | 15 |
| #6 | 0:24 | 2 | 0:24 | 2 | 0:24 | 2 | 1:12 | 6 |
| #7 | 0:48 | 4 | 0:48 | 4 | 1:24 | 7 | 3:00 | 15 |
| #8 | 0:48 | 4 | 0:48 | 4 | 1:36 | 8 | 3:12 | 16 |
| #9 | 0:48 | 4 | 0:48 | 4 | 1:48 | 9 | 3:24 | 17 |
| #10 | 0:48 | 4 | 0:48 | 4 | 2:00 | 10 | 3:36 | 18 |
| #11 | 0:36 | 3 | 0:36 | 3 | 1:12 | 6 | 2:24 | 12 |
| #12 | 0:24 | 2 | 0:24 | 2 | Half Marathon | 13.1 | 0:48+ | 4 + 13.1 |

# 10

# Marathon Training

MANY RUNNERS FIND that training for a marathon, and then completing one, represents a peak life experience. Some enjoy it so much that they run hundreds of marathons. Others are content with the once-and-done approach.

That's fine. There's no argument to be made that marathon running is essential to anyone's health and running routine. Palaeo runners didn't scratch two lines 26.2 miles apart in the African soil, and then time their attempts to bridge the two lines. Indeed, they never ran 26.2 miles non-stop.

Nor does anyone need to run marathons today. Even if you, like so many, want to lose weight, you don't need to run marathons. In fact, it's easier to lose weight through running when you are not training for a marathon, with its need for long-run fuelling.

The modern marathon exists primarily because we crave challenge and excitement in our lives. The man behind the London Marathon once called his event a 'suburban Everest' – a place where regular townsfolk could face a daunting physical endeavour without the trouble, expense, and life threats of an actual Everest expedition. This is a good thing, by the way, and largely explains why marathons have become a worldwide urban phenomenon.

At the end of this chapter, I've created a marathon plan you can follow or adapt to your needs. You won't find a simpler marathon plan anywhere. That's my programme's main strength. For example, you only have to run three days a week, and those days are always the same (unless you want to move them around from week to week, which is fine). The plan assumes only that you can run and walk 2 miles on the first day of training. From there, it builds slowly, sanely, and progressively.

Simple though my plan is, it's also 95 percent as thorough as the most demanding marathon plan. It covers the same main points – building weekly mileage, and increasing the length of your long run. The missing 5 percent is the number and distance of those long runs.

My plan only takes you to a long run of 18 miles, and you only do one of these. That means you will have to run slowly and conservatively on race day, probably with a mix of running and walking. The last 8 miles won't come easy. But you'll get through them, because the training has made you strong enough to endure, and your race-day motivation will do the rest.

Marathon race days are special. They shine a spotlight on the tremendous power of the human will. They show that we can achieve much more than what seemed possible just a short period earlier.

**Run by time:** Other marathon training plans give you mileage goals. My plan gives you time goals (hours and minutes), the same as *Run Forever*'s beginning running plan on page 19. Time goals are simpler and more precise than distance goals. You only have to run until X minutes have elapsed on your watch – there's nothing more to think about.

My plan assumes that you are running at about 12 minutes per mile. You might be faster or slower. Doesn't make a difference. Both will get you to the finish line. Also, I have put distances in miles in parentheses after each run.

**Take care of the small stuff:** When you're training for a marathon, your long-run days are central to your eventual success. Try to get them right. But pay attention to the small stuff too: sleep, diet, hydration, cross-training, and recovery. The whole is greater than the sum of the parts. It all adds up. Here's rule number one in marathon training: Get to the starting line as strong and healthy as possible.

**Expect bad days. Remember the good ones:** Everyone has bad days during a marathon build-up. Days when you will feel tired, and stressed, and reach the conclusion that you can not possibly finish your target marathon. Don't worry about these days.

Instead, reflect on the days when you feel fresh and strong. There is no fakery in running. Your good days give a true indication of your fitness and potential. You will have a good day during your marathon race, because you will be in great shape and fully rested for the big event.

# Beginner's Marathon Training Plan (16 weeks)

THIS PLAN ASSUMES that you can run or run-walk for about 24 minutes (roughly 2 miles) on day one. Your pace stays the same while your time and distance build slowly and progressively over 16 weeks.

You will probably find it most convenient to schedule your running for the same three days of every week (for example, Tuesday-Thursday-Saturday), but feel free to adjust.

| Week | Day 1 | | Day 2 | | Day 3 | | Week Totals | |
|---|---|---|---|---|---|---|---|---|
| | Running Time | Approx. Miles | Running Time | Approx. Miles | Running Time | Approx. Miles | Time (hours:minutes) | Miles |
| #1 | 0:24 | 2 | 0:24 | 2 | 0:36 | 3 | 1:24 | 7 |
| #2 | 0:24 | 2 | 0:24 | 2 | 0:48 | 4 | 1:36 | 8 |
| #3 | 0:36 | 3 | 0:36 | 3 | 0:60 | 5 | 2:12 | 11 |
| #4 | 0:36 | 3 | 0:36 | 3 | 1:12 | 6 | 2:24 | 12 |

| Week | Day 1 | | Day 2 | | Day 3 | | Week Totals | |
|---|---|---|---|---|---|---|---|---|
| | Running Time | Approx. Miles | Running Time | Approx. Miles | Running Time | Approx. Miles | Time (hours:minutes) | Miles |
| **#5** | 0:48 | 4 | 0:48 | 4 | 1:24 | 7 | 3:00 | 15 |
| **#6** | 0:48 | 4 | 0:48 | 4 | 1:36 | 8 | 3:12 | 16 |
| **#7** | 1:00 | 5 | 1:00 | 5 | 1:48 | 9 | 3:48 | 19 |
| **#8** | 0:48 | 4 | 0:48 | 4 | 0:48 | 4 | 2:24 | 12 |
| **#9** | 1:00 | 5 | 1:00 | 5 | 2:00 | 10 | 4:00 | 20 |
| **#10** | 1:12 | 6 | 1:12 | 6 | 2:24 | 12 | 4:48 | 24 |
| **#11** | 1:12 | 6 | 1:12 | 6 | 2:48 | 14 | 5:12 | 26 |
| **#12** | 1:00 | 5 | 1:00 | 5 | 1:00 | 5 | 3:00 | 15 |
| **#13** | 1:24 | 7 | 1:24 | 7 | 3:12 | 16 | 6:00 | 30 |
| **#14** | 1:00 | 5 | 1:00 | 5 | 3:36 | 18 | 5:36 | 28 |
| **#15** | 0:48 | 4 | 0:48 | 4 | 2:00 | 10 | 3:36 | 18 |
| **#16** | 0:24 | 2 | 0:24 | 2 | **Marathon** | 26.2 | 0:48 | 4 + 26.2 |

# SECTION 4

# DEALING WITH INJURIES

# Learning the Hard Way

I DON'T KNOW if *Run Forever* has improved your running – I certainly hope it has – but I can now say for certain that it has helped mine. Here's what happened. Two months ago, as I was beginning the final long push to complete the manuscript for this book, I suffered my first injury in seven years.

I'll tell you more about the injury in a few moments. At this point, the most salient detail is a word about my prior history in the injury-recovery department: sad. Depressing. Nothing to crow about. I have been far too impatient. Impulsive even. I have caused further injury when the goal is gradual healing.

As a sophomore in college, I suffered a stress fracture to a metatarsal of my left foot. It just happened one day while I was running. A similar injury is so common among army recruits in basic training that it has been given the name 'march fracture'. Not because it happens in the month between February and April, but because it strikes new recruits while they are going through various marching drills. It's an overuse injury, plain and simple.

Also, it's common and uncomplicated. It took my doc about 30 seconds to figure it out. And to prescribe my treatment. I didn't need to hobble around on crutches. I didn't need to have my foot immobilised in a cast. I only had to stop running and other serious exercise for six weeks. Small toe and metatarsal fractures, like the one I had, heal themselves.

If you let them. Unfortunately, I managed to follow the doctor's orders for just twenty-four hours. At that point in my running career, I was so driven to progress and improve that I would let almost nothing stand in my way. On the second day after my doctor visit, I started running again. I found that I could twist my left foot so absurdly that I put pressure only on the outer edge, not on the bottom. In this manner, I avoided metatarsal pain.

Somehow I persisted in this manner, running 5 to 8 miles a day, for ten days. I thought I was making progress. Until the day my foot exploded in pain mid-run. By the time I got home, it had ballooned in size, and turned a very-swollen black and blue. I could barely tug my shoe off.

Now I had no choice but to stop running entirely, and take six weeks off. During that time, my foot healed perfectly, and I trained myself back to top shape in just three to four weeks of renewed running.

Several years later I injured my gluteus maximus (butt muscle) by running a 3,000-meter steeplechase race I hadn't trained for. The next day, I couldn't lift my left (hurdling) leg out of bed. I should have rested this injury for several weeks as well, but the Olympic Marathon Trials were coming up in two months. I felt that I needed to train hard almost every day.

For that reason, my glute never healed, and I had to drop out of the Trials race. This effectively ended my Olympic dream. It was the biggest blow of my entire running career.

As I mentioned at the beginning of this essay, I've got an injury now. I'm happy to report that it didn't come from a training error or another stupid mistake. I simply stubbed a toe in a local trail run. I hit the offending rock hard enough to pitch forward, and fall at the side of the trail. Luckily, I landed in soft grass. No knee or hip or elbow injuries from the fall.

But for the rest of the run, I noticed a throbbing at the fourth toe of my right foot. It continued after I got home and iced the area. Three days later, after more ice and ibuprofen, the toe seemed no better. I didn't feel a sharp pain – not like what I remembered from that march fracture in college. But it continued throbbing. When I placed pressure on the toe, as when walking on it and pushing off into the next stride, it spoke to me loud and plain: 'That doesn't feel good. Please don't do it any more.'

So I didn't. I rode my recumbent bike at home, because I could do that with a flat, unflexed foot that produced no pain signals. I went to the gym three times a week to increase my strength training. I can always use more of that. After several weeks, I found that I could exercise hard on an elliptical machine, because, like the recumbent, it didn't force me to flex the toe and push off.

I hope you can tell that I'm patting myself on the back. For once, I was practising what I have always preached, and what I have written about in the pages that follow. It gets better.

After three weeks, when the toe was still more reactive than I would have expected, I decided to get an x-ray. Better safe than sorry, right? The x-ray proved completely clean. The radiologist couldn't detect any small fracture, or even any pooling of fluid as around a serious injury.

This made me mad for a moment. I thought: If there's nothing wrong with the damn foot, then I'm going to jump back into my training routine. For once, however, I listened to my body – I listened to the signals coming from the farthest reach of my body. The toe still hurt. It didn't want me to start running yet.

But now it said that walking would be okay. A small step forward. I called a friend who had just walked from San Francisco to Mexico, and scheduled several pleasant 60-minute walks with him. I also began entering 5K fun-runs, and walked the entire distance, aiming for 15:00 pace. I almost but not quite hit my goal.

Two weeks later I did my first run-walk. I covered 2 miles with a 1:1 ratio. My toe felt fine – no pain. I decided to repeat the same workout three times that week, and each of the following four weeks. I would progress from 1 mile to 2 to 4 to 6 to 8, always with the same 1:1 ratio.

I've just completed my first 8-miler. Because I'm getting back in the groove, it felt better than the first 2-miler. That's the way a running comeback should feel. You get smoother, easier, stronger all at the same time. In the next month, I'll gradually ratchet up the run-walk ratio. In two months, I expect to be running at almost full strength again.

Here's what I've learned from this process:

1) Many running injuries are caused by accidents, and not necessarily training errors. Be careful when trail running (or moving the furniture around your house).
2) Listen to your body. It's your best and most skilled physician.
3) There are many varieties of cross-training, and you can find several to keep you fit while you're injured.
4) Most importantly, the return to regular running must be very slow and gradual. You can't go wrong by leaning in the direction of extra caution.

The Rolling Stones sang that: 'Time, time, time is on my side. Yes it is.' The words turn out to be true for runners recovering from injury. You only have to give time free rein to work its magic.

# 1

# The Injury Conundrum

RUNNERS GET INJURED. There, I said it. Now let's move on to the larger truth: Few of these injuries are serious. Most runners soon return to their regular training routine with no permanent loss from the wear-and-tear they have endured.

How do I know this? Here's my argument. Marathon races are so popular these days that most entrants have to register six to nine months in advance. That's plenty of time to get injured and stop running. However, roughly 90 percent of marathon entrants actually show up on the start line of their races. Of those, more than 95 percent reach the finish.

This doesn't sound much like an epidemic of injured runners on crutches or in surgery. In fact, it's more like testimony to the grit, determination, and healthy running that describes most marathoners. They may falter, but they rarely fail.

Studies keep claiming that anywhere from 40 to 60 percent of runners get injured in a calendar year. Maybe there's some truth to that. It all depends on your definition of 'injury'. If you're including a sore muscle that requires a day or two of icing, the numbers climb. However, if you define injury as something that demands six weeks in a cast, the percentage drop precipitously.

It's no wonder that the same studies can't unlock what causes running injuries. They point a finger at only two consistent factors: prior injury, and high mileage. Everything else, amazingly, is unproven, including speed work and frequent racing. A long list of injury-recovery techniques are likewise mostly unproven: orthotics, massage, chiropractic, physical therapy, stretching, and all manner of special equipment.

I'm not trying to fill you with despair. Quite the opposite. As I noted in the example of the frequent marathon entrants and finishers, I believe there's good reason to feel optimistic about running injuries. Here's why: The vast majority involve soft-tissue complaints.

These usually melt away after several days or weeks. In other sports, you can break a bone or suffer wrenching knee or shoulder tears. These may require surgery, and will certainly demand a long, slow recovery. You might never return to your former strength and range of motion. Runners are rarely afflicted with these sorts of serious injuries. We bounce back quickly.

**Don't catastrophise:** Runners are so disciplined and determined (and maybe a bit control-freaky) that we too often despair when we get injured. We torment ourselves with worry that the injury will cause us to lose everything – all the training, all the goals, all the commitments to join others on race day. This rarely happens.

Injuries force us to re-evaluate and improvise a bit. We need to stay flexible. No, we're not going to be able to do every long run on the 16-week training schedule. But, yes, there's still time to recover and run strong.

Don't panic. You didn't just lose your best friend, or learn that you had a rapidly-spreading cancer. You lost five days of training due to a sprained ankle. In all likelihood, you'll be back on the roads in almost no time at all.

**Come back slowly:** The biggest mistake an injured runner can make is to return too soon to normal training. That's how minor injuries develop into longer-lasting and more severe ones. Take your time. Mix walking and very short, very slow runs. Build up cautiously. Any days you lose now will be like nothing compared to the many you would lose with a more serious condition.

**The pause that refreshes:** Injuries often have an unexpected outcome: You run better after you recover. This occurs when the injury forced you to rest from an overtraining period, and it happened to me in 1968. I won the Boston Marathon, but then dropped out of the Olympic Marathon Trials several months later with a nagging injury. Facing the pressure of the Trials, I had refused to rest and recover (as I now know I should have).

Depressed by my Trials failure, I went home and lay on the beach for the last two weeks of August. I did nothing. Then I accepted an invitation to a big new September race in Canada. I won the 12-miler handily, defeating a Canadian star who went on to place 10th in the Olympic Marathon a month later. The very Olympic Marathon I wasn't running due to my stupid obstinacy and refusal to rest an injury.

There is more life and running after an injury. Plenty of it.

# 2

# Training Errors

AS RUNNERS WE quite naturally look outside ourselves to place blame for our injuries. We think: It must be the shoes. Or maybe there's a special stretch or strengthening exercise no one has told me about yet. Perhaps I need to change my diet somehow – to hydrate more, or to consume more protein.

Sure, situations like the above could contribute to injury. But orthopaedists, podiatrists, physical therapists, and other experts have a different view. They believe runners cause running injuries. We inflict them on ourselves.

How? Through training errors. We do too much, too soon, too fast, too many hills, and so on. We push the body beyond its break point, and guess what? It breaks.

When speaking at running seminars, I often say, 'The first smart runner hasn't been born yet.' That's meant to be a joke, as runners are highly thoughtful and educated. I'm simply trying to make an important point. We tend to repeat the training errors of those who have come before us, and warned us. Just as I'm doing with you now. We find it nearly impossible to absorb the wisdom of all the injured runners who have preceded us.

There's a reason for this. When you've been running smoothly and effortlessly for several months or even years, you can't imagine that the next mile could put you in peril. But it could. Especially if you've been pushing your luck by running farther, faster, or more often.

Runners need to understand an important paradox: That which makes us stronger also makes us weak. It can lead to injuries. Here's how the paradox works.

As a general truth, runners are incredibly productive individuals. We set goals, and work hard to reach them. We don't let minor stumbling blocks get in the way. We push onward. This approach often leads to great success, not just in our running, but also in many other areas of life – from art to academics, to our professional careers, to our community and family lives.

However, the same discipline can backfire when it comes to running injuries. You can't ignore them, and you can't just persevere through them. In fact, it's much smarter to briefly reverse your normal can-do attitude.

**Listen to pain:** Pain is a subjective experience, precisely why so many runners ignore it, and stick to their training schedule. Instead, they shunt the pain signals to a distant corner of the brain, where the message is barely perceived.

Don't do this. When you feel acute discomfort while running, acknowledge it. And begin to formulate a recovery plan. Try to evaluate the depth of the pain. Is it sharp, or is it dull? Does it go away as you warm up into a run, or get worse? A sharp pain that hurts more every mile is a clear warning. Stop at once. Get home however you can, and start taking action. A dull ache or tightness may be less serious, but also deserves attention.

'I worry about pain, because it tends to change a runner's mechanics,' says Jordan Metzl, MD, author of *Running Strong*. 'And changed mechanics can lead to more serious problems.'

**Take several days off:** Unless you're a gold-medal contender in an upcoming Olympic Games, don't try to train through an injury. That path too often spirals down a deep, dark hole.

Start with rest. There's no precise number that covers all situations, but take two to three days with no running. None. At all. Whenever possible throughout the day, apply 10 minutes of ice to the injured area. You can take an over-the-counter anti-inflammatory for as long as seven to ten days. If your injury is a relatively minor soft-tissue strain – the most common of injuries – several days of no running might put you back on the road.

Walking is the best medicine, as long as you can walk without pain. Otherwise, this is a time for caution and chilling out. Don't take a new yoga class, or mimic an internet stretching video. Save those activities until you have regained full strength.

**Tear up the calendar:** Unless you're lucky, you can't get injured and reach your next short-term goal at the same time. Don't try. You can nail that goal in a subsequent training cycle. Concentrate instead on the joy of returning to pain-free running.

Run much slower and shorter than normal. Take walking breaks as necessary. Use ice or massage or other preferred therapies after each run. Relax. Running is a gift, and now is a good time to appreciate it.

# 3

# Cross Training

WHEN CROSS TRAINING and triathlon races first made a big splash in the 1980s, I worried that running would somehow tail off. I feared it might prove a fad, with many participants moving on to the next big thing. Now I hold the exact opposite opinion.

Cross-training has done more to encourage and assist lifetime runners than any other movement. Heck, I do it myself, plenty of it. Half my weekly workouts don't require that I lace up running shoes. Instead, I read newspapers and magazines while pedalling my recumbent bike.

I enjoy and endorse athletic congregations – people coming together from diverse beginning points. One hundred and fifty years ago in England, a few hardy souls began 'hares and hounds' foot races across Wimbledon Common. A decade later Captain Matthew Webb became the first to swim the English Channel. The Oxford–Cambridge rowing race got started about thirty years earlier.

The Tour de France was first held in 1903. Nordic skiing existed in distant, frigid parts of the globe. In 1972, Title IX opened the doors to female athletes. The more, the merrier, as far as I'm concerned.

With the massive popularity of the Hawaii Ironman on TV, people who had begun running in the 1970s rediscovered the cobweb-covered bicycles in their basements. Skinny runners learned how to swim. Health clubs popped up on almost every urban block, and aerobic dance classes put bodies in sweaty, rhythmic motion. Lifting weights made you fitter for any activity.

All these options proved particularly attractive to the 95 percent of runners who never won a medal or prize at weekend races. Why put all your eggs in one basket when you could have more fun in many activities?

Best of all, cross training reduces injuries. If you don't push a single effort to an extreme, you get stronger and fitter across the board. You don't suffer from repetitive, overuse injuries. This is monumentally important. A healthy, uninjured athlete is one who can continue his/her healthy activities for life. Which is the name of the game.

**Take a seat:** Most runners use cross-training to recover from recent workouts, or to heal from injury. That means you should get off your feet. Indoor and outdoor bicycles offer the most popular options, but water activities also provide a great medium. You can sit in a boat or rowing machine, run in a pool (with a floatation vest, so your feet never touch the bottom), or of course swim in a pool or open water.

Runners tend to make lousy swimmers. I'm talking about myself here. We think we can just grit it out and get better, as we did in running. This rarely works. Water is such a thick, resistant medium (unlike air) that good technique makes a huge difference. I'll always be a sub-par swimmer, but I improved substantially after I sought out a good coach.

My appreciation also soared. Now, when I get out of the water after about 15 minutes, my body feels as loose and content as it does after a massage.

**Get on your feet:** To use cross-training to enhance your running speed versus recovery, you have to move much as you do when running. You have to get on your feet, and rotate one in front of the other. This is the classic 'specificity of training' rule at work.

Several decades ago, you could only do this while riding uphill on a bicycle. Now the local health club has dozens of new machines that work great for runners, including steppers, and a range of elliptical trainers. I often find that I can use these even when injured, as the smooth, rotational footpads eliminate road pounding. Just be sure to let pain and discomfort guide you. Cross-training is no bonus if your feet or legs still hurt. In that case, you're just extending an injury.

**Train like a triathlete:** Once an extreme oddity, the triathlon is now a bona-fide Olympic event, and a great test of all-round endurance. Many runners have made triathlon training a part of their regular routine, especially in summer.

Some have even improved their running while doing less of it, due to the time they spend on the other two activities. This isn't true for everyone, but it's more common than you might expect. These individuals get better because they focus more on each of their fewer, shorter, faster running workouts. They narrow their run training, and become more efficient at it.

# 4

# Stretching and Strengthening

TO STRETCH OR not to stretch, that is the question. It has always been the question. I first heard about various legs stretches at high-school cross-country practice in 1962. The stretching din has only increased since then, as more runners took up the sport, found themselves injured at times, and looked to stretching for a cure.

Unfortunately, it isn't. Countless studies have failed to uncover a link between stretching and injury prevention. In fact, some have reached the opposite conclusion – that stretching contributes to injuries. Moreover, research indicates that greater flexibility does not lead to faster performances. It may point the other way.

These conclusions strike many as incredible, as if someone proposed that eating a large meal would not reduce your hunger. I'm not one of the disbelievers, however. I see the logic – the possible explanation.

Stretching is supposed to improve flexibility, and it does. But flexibility isn't necessarily a good thing for runners. Consider one of its synonyms – 'instability'. You wouldn't want to have an unstable knee or foot. These are associated with injuries.

In running, we strive to minimise extra motion. Less is more. If your running stride includes a lot of sway or wasted motion, you can't possibly run smoothly, efficiently, and fast.

Many top runners perform with an almost mechanical precision. I picture 2014 Boston Marathon winner Meb Keflezighi with his short, metronomic stride. He runs with no wasted motion, and no lower-body sway. All his energy is directed toward powering straight ahead.

Unlike stretching, strength work has the potential to decrease injuries and increase efficiency. Research has shown that strengthening the muscles around the knee lowers the risk of knee injury, as does hip-abductor strengthening.

Strength training also improves running economy, and hence running performance. A 2016 systematic review and meta-analysis in the *Journal of Conditioning Research* concluded: 'A strength training programme performed two to three times a week is an appropriate strategy to improve running economy in highly trained middle- and long-distance runners.'

**Don't stretch *before* running:** If you stretch before running, you risk injury. This is especially true if your leg muscles have not warmed up yet. The best and safest way to get ready for running is with a gentle walk that transitions to a slow jog, and then to your normal pace.

Stretching before races has been shown to decrease performance. Runners used to think that stretching would give them more range of motion – that is, a longer stride. However, physiologists now believe that stretching reduces the natural elasticity and energy-return of the body's dynamic tissues. These include the tendons, ligaments, and muscles.

**If you enjoy stretching, do it *after* a run:** Many runners use their stretching time as a relaxing and pleasurable part of the day. If you're one of these, fine. But save your stretching until after you run. Or until later in the day when your leg muscles are fully warmed up. The morning is the worst time for stretching.

Some runners stretch while watching the nightly news or other TV. You can lie on the floor, and casually perform your favourite routine without feeling the pressures of the day. One of my friends does this for 45 minutes every night. He wouldn't give it up for anything. And he's almost never injured.

**Make time for strength training:** The American College of Sports Medicine, and fitness experts everywhere preach the value of strength training at least twice a week. Most women are naturally less strong than most men – no offence meant, ladies – and should pay particular attention to building and maintaining their strength. The same goes for aging men and women.

Runners should focus on strength-training the quadriceps, glutes, hamstrings, and calf muscles to limit injuries, and improve performance. At the same time, whole-body strengthening routines will boost your health and well-being, so don't skimp on the core and upper body.

# 5

# Shin Splints

IF THERE'S A nearly universal running injury, it is surely shin splints. I can recall few beginning runners who didn't suffer from this general shin-pain condition at some point in their first weeks of regular training. That sounds ominous. But virtually all runners manage to treat their shin splints, recover, and move on to more ambitious running goals. Shin splints are never a game-over situation. They're not a reason to quit running altogether.

You might hear a doctor or physical therapist refer to shin splints as 'medial tibial stress syndrome'. That's because the shin bone is named the tibia, and the pain is usually felt on the inner (medial) side of the shin. You'll notice the aggravation with each foot strike while running, and also afterward, since the inflammation alongside the tibia continues even when you have stopped running.

Like most running injuries, shin splints are caused by overuse. In this case, it's an almost inevitable overuse. When you go from no running to some running, you dramatically increase the forces on your lower legs. If you are young, lean, and relatively fit, your muscles and bone attachments may accommodate the new activity.

However, if you are older, not so lean, and not so fit, your legs will object. They'll need time to adjust and grow stronger. During this period of gradually increasing fitness, you might develop shin splints.

A small minority of runners suffer from repetitive bouts of shin splints. Most don't. Once you move past an initial bout of shin splints, they rarely come back (unless you return to running after a long lay-off).

Shin splints are the perfect example of why most running injuries aren't serious. You get them, then you get over them. Yes, they are unpleasant. Sure, they will probably force a re-evaluation of your training plan, and several weeks of less running with more rehabilitation. But that should be the end of it. So don't panic, and don't lose confidence.

**Change your running programme:** In most cases, you could stick to your training plan with shin splints. The aching is more an aggravation than a sharp pain. But why bother continuing?

The point of lifelong running is to establish an exercise routine that you actually enjoy. Running in pain is not the way to go. So downshift your training goals. Treat your shin splints by taking several days to a week off. When you start up again, run slower, shorter, and less frequently.

While recovering, try any cross-training that doesn't bother your shins. You'll probably do fine with strength training, and water activities. There's a good chance that walking, bicycling, rowing, and elliptical workouts won't irritate your shins. Give them a whirl. Back off, and switch to another activity if necessary.

**Treat the inflammation:** Shin splints respond well to regular icing. Apply an ice pack or frozen peas to your shins as often as you can during the day, up to five or six times. Leave the ice on for 10 to 15 minutes, no longer. In particular, apply ice immediately after completing a cross-training workout. Using an NSAID for shin splints will limit the inflammation, but don't continue for more than seven to ten days.

You can support the muscles around your shins by wrapping them in athletic tape or one of the many silicone or neoprene 'sleeves' that have hit the market. These may decrease the forces on the tibia (the big shin bone), and help you recover from the achy feeling. They also provide a good physical and psychological crutch when you begin to increase your weekly mileage again.

Strengthen the shins: There are a number of simple, popular, and effective exercises that gradually increase your shin-muscle strength. Don't attempt these when your shin splints are at their most painful. Wait until you are on the road to recovery.

First, while standing barefoot with your back against a wall (for support), lift your toes and forefeet toward your shins. Keep your heels firmly planted on the floor, and your knees straight. Start with just half a dozen, and gradually increase. Second, sit in a chair with your feet on a towel on the floor. 'Scrunch' your toes and forefeet to pull the towel toward you. Do a dozen or so scrunches to begin, and build up.

# 6

# Knee Injuries

CONTRARY TO WHAT many believe, runners suffer no more from knee injuries and knee arthritis than the general population. In fact, runners may have fewer knee problems. A 2017 report in *Arthritis Care & Research* investigated the question, looking at more than 2,600 adults. The researchers found that the runners had 24 percent less knee osteoarthritis than the non-runners.

There's a reason why the runner's knee is so resilient: We were born to run. The knee joint has literally evolved to assist simple forward and backward tracking of the lower leg. We walk and we run. No problem. (But beware knee-torquing sports like skiing, tennis, and basketball.) Runners also have healthy knees because we build muscle around the joint, and carry little excess weight on the rest of our frame.

Of course this doesn't stop runners from worrying about the knees more than any other part of the leg. Every runner experiences some knee pain at one time or another. And we know too many who have quit running due to knee pain. This fills us with fear and trepidation.

The knee isn't soft tissue that can heal itself in a matter of days. It's a complex joint where major bones, muscle groups, and support structures come together. And, no doubt about it, the knee absorbs substantial shock and strain when we run. Occasionally, some part of the knee gives out.

I count myself among the knee-injured runners. In 2010, I had meniscus-repair surgery at the left knee. The injury occurred when I ran a half-marathon despite several prior days of distinct pain at the knee. Stupid, I know. I was past sixty, and worried that my running days might be near their end.

Not even close. Four months after surgery and appropriate recovery and training, I completed the 2010 Athens Marathon. That was the one that celebrated the 2,500th anniversary of Pheidippides's run from Marathon to Athens. My left knee felt good as new.

It has carried me through five straight Boston Marathons since Athens, and every other run and race I've chosen to enter. When you treat the body well, it has amazing recuperative powers.

**Don't over-stride:** Over-striding is the most common form mistake made by runners. A long stride is necessary for sprinters, but the wrong approach for distance runners. You know you're over-striding when your front foot strikes the ground ahead of a plumb line dropped straight down from the knee.

This does two bad things. First, it increases the shock forces that flash up your leg to your knee and hips. Second, it puts the knee in a bad position to use its surrounding muscles and other support structures.

Instead, aim for a comfortably short stride, more of a shuffle than a pogo-stick bounding effort. With this stride, you'll land under your knee (not in front of it) in the perfect position to utilise your powerful knee muscles.

**Try different shoes:** Some runners have resolved their knee issues by switching to minimalist (barefoot-like) running shoes, and/or severely shortening their stride to land on the forefeet instead of the heels. A number of studies have pointed to biomechanical reasons that might explain why and how this works.

But the minimalist approach carries its own risks. It may increase the chances of calf, Achilles, ankle, and foot injuries. I recommend that you try minimalist shoes only if you have exhausted all other therapies. In that case, why not? Be sure you transition to minimalist running slowly and cautiously.

**Avoid hills:** Uphill and downhill running both make the knee muscles do double the work of flatland running. Avoid them if you have knee pain. Stick to flat roads or a running track, often the best place to renew running after an injury.

Many runners with achy knees find relief on trails and grass, which are, after all, softer than asphalt roads. Since these surfaces are uneven, they demand a shorter, nimbler stride – a good thing on its own. Boston Marathon legend Bill Rodgers stays off the roads as much as he can these days. 'I've enjoyed running on grass ever since high school,' he says. 'Now that I'm in my late sixties, I definitely think it helps.'

**Strength train:** Research consistently shows that strength training can promote healthier knees that are less likely to develop an injury. Concentrate on the quadriceps and hip abductors. There are many simple routines, using equipment or only your own body weight, to strengthen these two muscle groups. Stronger muscles help the bones track straight and true through the joint, without excessive wobble or instability.

# 7

# Achilles Tendinitis

I AM MORE frightened of Achilles tendon injuries than any other. For good reason. In my early fifties, I suffered through a three-year period when calf and especially Achilles strains regularly thwarted my running.

I never knew when the next pull would occur. Some struck in the middle of hard races, but most came on typical, easy-day runs. I've never had another time in my long running career when I was so exasperated.

I visited a series of medical professionals, chiropractors to physical therapists. All could see the problem. My right Achilles tendon was red, swollen, and painful to the touch. It even made a creaking sound – honest, it's called 'crepitus' – caused by friction rubbing within the tendon sheath.

I tried various treatments, some of which helped for a week or two. Then my leg would seize up again, unexpectedly, on a slow, conservative run. After several years, my podiatrist said he was 90 percent certain I would need surgery if I wished to continue running.

I did, but I was 99 percent sure I didn't want surgery. I kept trying various self-help techniques for Achilles tendinitis. I also endured extended periods of little to no running.

Eventually something clicked. I wish I could tell you exactly what it was. But the truth is, I don't know. I only know that the tendinitis subsided, and I've since enjoyed two decades of healthy running with no Achilles complaints. I learned what I've been telling other runners ever since: Most injuries resolve themselves at some point, just not as soon as we would like. Be patient.

An important Achilles tendon note for runners: In 2016, the FDA issued a 'Drug Safety Communication' concerning the link between tendinitis, especially Achilles tendinitis, and a class of antibiotics known as fluoroquinolones. At least one widely-prescribed antibiotic, Cipro, belongs to the fluoroquinolones. If you are prescribed Cipro (full name: ciproflaxin) by your doctor, make sure he or she knows you are a runner. Ask if you can be put on a different antibiotic.

**Stop running:** The sooner you stop running after noticing unusual Achilles pain, the faster you are likely to heal. Achilles injuries only get worse when you continue to run on them. Hilly courses and speed work are especially troublesome.

Instead, rest, ice the afflicted area, and take an NSAID for no longer than seven to ten days. Put a heel pad in your shoe so the Achilles won't be stretched by your normal walking and other activities. Don't begin stretching and strengthening exercises while your Achilles is in the acute injury phase. Wait until you feel that some healing has taken place.

**The sleep cure:** I said above that I'm not sure what led to the reversal of my Achilles tendon injury. That's true. But I believe one of the contributing treatments was sleeping in an ankle-Achilles brace. This device kept my calf and Achilles in a slightly stretched position for eight hours every night to facilitate healing. There are a number of inexpensive braces and socks designed to do this. They can't hurt, and they helped me get back on the road to recovery.

**Specific stretches and strength routines:** The strain on your Achilles tendon can be lessened by flexible calf muscles. The simplest, safest calf exercise is the wall stretch. Stand two feet away from a wall, put your hands on the wall, and incline forward, keeping your legs straight and your heels anchored on the floor. You'll feel the stretch from your ankles to the back of your knees.

When you're comfortable with this stretch, you can move to a more aggressive position, and perform the bent-knee wall stretch. It's the same as the above, except you put one foot in front of the other, about halfway to the wall. When you incline forward, bend the front knee, but keep the back knee straight. You'll feel an increased stretch in the lower part of the back leg.

Many runners with Achilles tendinitis have gotten good results from heel drops and raises. These are usually performed on a stairway. Put the front of your afflicted foot on the tread, with the heel extending beyond the edge of the step. Use the other foot on the tread for balance and support only.

Let the injured heel drop slowly, then raise it up beyond its starting position. Repeat the dropping and raising rotation, being sure to go slow, and maintain control of your movements. Start with a modest number of drops and raises. Increase only if you experience no pain.

# 8

# The Perils of Pain Pills

AT FIRST GLANCE, the group of common pain medications called NSAIDs (non-steroidal anti-inflammatory drugs) would seem to be a runner's dream come true. They mask minor aches and pains, and reduce inflammation. Runners have plenty of both. Ergo, a match made in heaven. The most common NSAIDs include aspirin, ibuprofen (such as Advil and Motrin) and naproxen (Aleve).

However, this group of widely-available pain pills deserves a second, closer scrutiny. Like all drugs, they have side-effects. Most runners don't think about the side-effects, because they never develop major problems. But a clear understanding of the risks is important for smart, healthy running.

NSAIDs can cause stomach upset and bleeding. They may interfere with kidney function. They have been shown to disrupt messenger proteins that contribute to the training effect (the reason you are running in the first place). And they are associated with increased risk of stroke and heart attack.

In fact, in 2015 the Food and Drug Administration toughened the language required on NSAID consumer-information labels. The labels now warn that 'the risk of heart attack or stroke can occur as early as the first weeks' of NSAID use, and can increase with continued use over longer periods of time. One NSAID researcher summed up her view as follows: 'Patients should use the smallest possible dose for the shortest possible time.'

That's a wonderful guideline, which I follow myself. Yes, I use NSAIDS on occasion. However, only when I have a specific, acute ache or pain, and never for more than seven to ten days in a row. That's what most experts recommend, and it seems the safe, prudent, smart approach.

Acetaminophen is a different story. It's an effective pain reliever that carries less heart risk than the NSAIDs, but it's not an anti-inflammatory. Hence, it's good for pain blocking but not injury healing. Use it accordingly. The National Institutes of Health recommend taking less than 4,000 milligrams a day, and not for an extended period.

**Don't pop pills:** According to some surveys, up to 70 percent of runners use NSAIDs at one time or another. If you're one of these, limit your use to acute, short-term situations. Don't get into the habit of tossing back a few pills before every workout or race. They're not an appropriate insurance policy against aches and pains.

In fact, they could backfire by masking a pain that needs more specialised attention.

The result could be a minor injury that turns into a bigger, more long-term one.

The up-and-down motion of running produces a sloshy stomach. That's why more runners than cyclists become nauseous while exercising, particularly if they hydrate a lot. The stomach sloshing also exacerbates an NSAID's tendency to increase intestinal leakage and systemic inflammation. The only things you should introduce to your stomach while running are fluids and fuel – not pain pills.

**Begin with RICE:** The classic RICE approach is the best way to begin tissue rehab: Rest, Ice, Compression, Elevation. Every runner I know has a bag of peas in the freezer to apply against various parts of the leg. I put my peas inside a plastic sandwich bag to give my skin a secondary layer of protection from the ice.

Recently, some physical therapists have begun following the

PRICE system. The 'P' stands for 'protection'. It represents a strap, belt, and/or functional compression sleeve that can be worn around the clock, including your first cautious return to exercise. I have several of these with adjustable Velcro straps that I can adjust to my leg circumference.

**Opt for non-pill relief:** We runners have an ever-growing selection of alternative therapies for pain relief when dealing with muscle and tissue discomfort. As a general rule, these are far safer and smarter than NSAID use. The therapies include ice, cold water, massage, acupressure, acupuncture, trigger-point therapy, and self-massage with a range of sticks, rollers, and similar devices.

Some are more effective for one type of injury than for another, but all are employed by large numbers of runners. I have a handful of self-massage, self-pressure tools that I use when necessary. They sit idle much of the time, thank goodness, but I find them effective at relieving the discomfort of minor injuries.

# 9

# Blisters

RUNNERS MOVE. A LOT. Our feet move, our thighs move, our arms and shoulders move. These body parts are covered by shoes or clothing, and when the material rubs against naked skin, as it inevitably must, the result is increased friction. Friction is no friend to runners. It causes heat, blisters, burns, and rashes.

Most blisters turn out to be temporary annoyances. They certainly don't lead to long-term health issues. This doesn't make them a minor problem, however. I've dropped out of more races due to blisters than any other injury. The total isn't high – less than a handful, in fact – but that's more than my drop-outs due to knee injuries, Achilles tendinitis, dehydration, and the like.

That's why every runner needs a programme designed to prevent blisters. Start with your shoes. They cause the most damaging and long-lasting blisters. Don't purchase shoes that are either too tight or too loose.

You might think that snug-fitting shoes are essential. Not so. Your feet will expand when you run, especially on warm days. Most experts suggest you buy shoes with a thumbnail's width of space between your toes and the front of your shoes.

Overly large shoes are just as troublesome. Your feet will slip and slide too much in them, creating movement and friction. Again, friction is not your friend. Don't encourage it.

Race days foster far more blisters than normal training, because racing is different and much more stressful. For starters, you might be wearing different shoes and clothes.

You also run faster, sweat more, and spend more time on hot black surfaces (asphalt). You might pour water over your head to cool down or run through a spray station. All these can contribute to blistering you haven't encountered in training.

If you're running a marathon, your total race times and miles are almost certainly higher than any training run. Before a marathon, you should triple-check your blister defences.

When you do get blisters, the American Dermatological Association suggests that you leave small ones alone to resolve on their own. Use a band aid or moleskin to decrease any discomfort you feel. Avoid popping blisters, as this could lead to infection.

However, if your blister is large and painful, follow this procedure: Sterilize a sharp needle with rubbing alcohol, then pierce the blister at one edge to drain the fluid. Don't pull off or cut off the skin that forms the blister's roof. Just wash with soap and water, and keep it clean.

**Vaseline, the wonder lubricant:** Vaseline is practically the original running product. I've seen it at every race I've run since 1962. Back then, menthol rubs were just as popular. The rubs have disappeared, but Vaseline remains, because it serves a basic purpose by providing a thin layer of goop to prevent friction. Don't leave home without it.

Vaseline works in exactly the way that it seems, coating the body with a protective gel that prevents friction and chafing of the skin. Other athletic-specific products like Body Glide do the same with less of a greasy feel. They also let the skin breathe, so that sweat can escape.

**Protect all delicate areas:** While the feet are prone to blisters, running causes movement, friction, and potential rash and bleeding to other body parts. These include the armpits, where sweat and swinging arms cause friction, and the thighs, which often rub against the liner of your shorts (or the opposite thigh). To avoid these, wear modern, breathable fabrics, and apply Vaseline or other salves.

Women wear bras, men don't. As a result, men are often afflicted by bleeding nipples. It's probably the grossest sight in running, and also agonisingly painful – the more so if you are running 26 miles. For protection, use Vaseline, or cover the nipples with band-aids or products specifically designed to prevent friction and bleeding. The precautionary care is well worth the effort.

**Choose great socks:** In my book, modern running socks are the single greatest advance of the last fifty years in running. You can have your heart monitors, chronographs, GPS watches, fitness trackers, and all the others. I'll take good running socks.

The cotton socks of my early running days trapped sweat like a sponge. If I happened to pour a little water over my head on a ninety-degree day, it would drip into my socks, and form a puddle. Sometimes I could hear my feet sloshing inside my socks.

All this moisture caused blisters, which produced pain and limping that sometimes led to a DNF (did not finish). Today's water-wicking socks are a thousand times better, and one of the few pieces of running equipment I'm willing to spend a few extra pounds on. I don't have a favourite. Rather, I enjoy trying new makes and models, and find that I appreciate just about all of them.

# 10

# A Proven Warm-Up Routine

I'VE NOTED PREVIOUSLY that the first evidence-based injury prevention programme has yet to be invented. Claims are made, but convincing proof is rarely advanced. Runners (and other athletes) get injured for a whole host of reasons – mainly, individual differences – that don't lend themselves to easy analysis. Finding a 'cure' is even more difficult.

Many injury studies suffer from a lack of verifiable information about the subjects' training methods. Just because someone self-reports that she runs 20 miles a week doesn't guarantee that she actually does. And when someone claims to attend yoga classes twice a week for an hour at a time, how can that be verified?

The use of self-report questionnaires is a widely-known weakness in exercise and nutrition studies. It's easy and inexpensive to collect reams of data with questionnaires, but the data is squishy – that is, ill-defined and undependable.

That's why I pay special attention to studies conducted by the military on military recruits. The army is highly motivated to prevent injuries and improve performance. When it fails, it squanders money, and may even diminish national security.

Importantly, the military recruits represent a captive audience as research subjects. The army 'owns' them for a period of time, and knows everything about them. The recruits don't fill out questionnaires. The data comes from drill sergeants and other instructors who actually observe everything the recruits do during a day. There is nothing squishy about the army or the data it collects.

In early 2017, a group of army researchers published their latest report on a warm-up routine that improves 2-mile run times and has the potential to decrease lower-leg injuries. The first outcome was statistically significant; the second was not. Nonetheless, it led to a positive trend that was impressive enough for me to begin using the warm-up myself.

The programme, called DIME (for 'Dynamic Integrated Movement Enhancement') includes ten basic exercises that take only 10 to 12 minutes in total to perform. Many are familiar to runners, while a few are not. Though the complete DIME warm-up is beyond the scope of this book, I can lay out the fundamentals.

**Bend those knees:** The DIME protocol includes both double-leg squats and forward lunges. In the former, you stand with your feet shoulder-width apart, and slowly lower your butt to sitting height, but not lower. Then slowly stand up again. Point your toes straight ahead, not to the side, and don't let your knees extend in front of your toes. Repeat ten times.

In the forward lunge, step forward with one foot, and bend the knee, allowing your butt to sink. Before the rear knee hits the ground, contract your front leg muscles to lift upward and move forward. Repeat the same motion with the other foot and leg leading the way. Keep your torso upright throughout, and don't bend either knee more than ninety degrees. Start with ten lunges, and build to a comfortable number.

**Get grounded:** Next, do push-ups and side planks. Everyone knows how to do push-ups. Focus on contracting the abs, and keeping your back straight. Aim for six to ten push-ups for starters.

To do a side plank, lie on your right side, supporting yourself on the right forearm with your feet resting one on top of the other. Tighten your abs and glutes, and raise your hips off the floor until they are in a straight line with your shoulders and feet. Hold for 20 to 30 seconds. Repeat three to five times on each side.

**Hippity-hop:** The most interesting and unique part of the DIME programme is its inclusion of three hopping movements. Here are two, starting with the side hop. Begin by balancing on one foot with a slightly-bent knee to engage muscles and avoid a stiff joint. Then hop sideways to the other foot, and find your balance there. Finish the exercise by hopping back to the original foot. Land as softly as possible. It's okay to bend forward at the hips. Go slow. Aim for six to ten hops, back and forth.

The second is called the L-R hop. Start on your left foot with your right knee slightly flexed so the foot is off the ground. Hop forward, then back to your start position, to the left, and back to the start. Repeat five times, landing softly. Switch to the right foot. Hop forward, back, to the right, and back. Repeat five times.

# SECTION 5

# GAINING SPEED

# Running the Gamut

I KNOW THAT great effort is required to achieve great things, and I don't shrink from such effort. In fact, I embrace it. I absorbed self-discipline very early from a hard-working, no-nonsense German mother. Sometimes I wonder if I learned too well.

This isn't always a bad thing. In endurance competitions, you need more determination than the racers who line up to your left and right. You need to train long, hard, and consistent. That's how you get ahead, how you reach your goals.

When it comes to speed training, however, the same doesn't apply. More isn't better. It took me a long time to learn this lesson.

In my first days of high-school cross-country, every run was filled with many surprises. We played follow-the-leader behind my coach, John Kelley. He started by scrambling over several stone walls adjacent to the high school, which sat at the top of a commanding hill. We scrambled after him. It was physical work, like clambering up a playground jungle gym.

Next Kelley frolicked through the twisting trails of Haley Farm, up hillside apple orchards, down the rocky, root-strewn paths to the edge of Long Island Sound. We followed, with quick feet, the only way to avoid tripping and falling. Reaching nearby Bluff Point State Park, we splashed through tidal inlets, scurried up the namesake bluff, and twisted right and left to avoid raspberry-bush scratches.

I don't remember ever getting tired during the first half of a run.

I was too busy tailing Kelley, and struggling to stay on my feet. The second half? Oh, yeah, I got plenty tired. Kelley had a special talent for picking up the pace imperceptibly. Every time we reached a slight hill, he surged ahead. Next hill, a little faster again.

By the time we clambered back over the thick stone walls where we had begun an hour earlier, my teammates and I were exhausted. We flopped onto the grass next to the baseball field, our chests heaving to pull in more oxygen. Running with Kelley was exhilarating, and strangely effective. Our team won a lot of cross-country titles.

In college, I learned about interval training. Plus I met a kindred spirit named Jeff Galloway, a distance runner from Atlanta. Jeff craved distance success as much as I did, and believed in long interval sessions.

One early October afternoon at Wesleyan University, the two of us set out to tackle forty x 400 metres with a 100-meter jog. We ran barefoot on a grass loop that circled the Wesleyan track and football field. Jeff timed every 400. Two years younger, I followed along like the young pupil I was.

I remember that the sun was high and warm when we started. Ten repeats. Still warm. Twenty. All good. Then the sun set behind Wesleyan's Foss Hill, and a chill settled upon us. The grass turned damp with dew, which sent a tingle through the bottoms of my feet. This was good. It kept me going.

We didn't talk. We just ran our 400s, round and round and round. We didn't once discuss the mounting fatigue. We didn't consider bailing out after twenty-five or thirty repeats. That would have been unthinkable. We had set our sights on forty, and, by God, we were going to do forty.

The next autumn, we repeated the same workout one more time. Then Jeff graduated and I had to train mostly on my own. I kept doing intervals, because I hoped to get faster. I enjoyed great success in cross-country – in fact, I didn't lose a dual meet in four years – but I sucked in track races. Almost anyone could outkick me on the last lap.

So I pushed the boundaries of interval training. One frigid day in January, I ran sixty x 200 metres on the Coast Guard Academy's new indoor track. One summer night, I returned to the barefoot approach, zipping back and forth down the centre of a local football field until I had accumulated seventy-two 100-yard sprints.

Stamina? You bet. And yet the speed never followed. I kept losing track races, and eventually grew tired of endless interval sessions. There had to be a better way.

In a moment of inspiration (or perhaps desperation) I thought: Why not try something less scripted, like the Haley Farm runs of my youth behind John Kelley?

Having moved back to Connecticut after several decades in Pennsylvania, I was even able to return to Haley Farm itself. I found it much improved from the scraggly paths I remembered, thanks to a local conservation group that had gained stewardship. There were more options now, but still the familiar stone walls, orchards, and hills.

I invented an entirely new workout, unlike anything I had ever heard about or read about. I thought it deserved a name, so I gave it one – 'frolics' – after the freeform running John Kelley had practised fifty years earlier.

My frolics workouts have three goals: First, they should be relatively short, not like endless intervals that go on for 90 minutes or more. Most of my frolics sessions last about 40 minutes. Second, they should make complete use of the available environment. Kelley scrambled this way and that, and my frolics workouts are similarly unscripted. Third, frolics are a time to run fast. They are a type of speed training.

Basically, I sprint up and down the Haley Farm hills, maybe 20 seconds at a time. Since I'm running fast, I need long recovery periods, so I walk several minutes between surges. When I pass a low stone wall, I pretend it's a steeplechase barrier. I approach at a steady pace, adjust my steps to jump onto the wall, land on top, push off, and sprint hard for 50 yards. Then I turn around to walk back, and repeat several more of these steeplechase simulations.

If I approach a taller stone wall, I don't attempt to jump it. Instead, I stop to do step-ups. I lift my forward knee high, step onto the wall, and then step off. I repeat this for 20 to 30 seconds, alternating my lifting leg, and then jog off to find a next encounter.

No two frolics sessions are ever the same, and they can't be quantified. But, believe me, my body tells me all I need to know. My legs complain for several days after. There's no doubt that I've put real effort and power into the routine.

At the same time, these workouts are short, lively, and fun. They remind me of yesteryear, when, as a teen, a hard cross-country run was like a romp through a playground.

Best of all, frolics seem to deliver a bigger pay-off than much longer interval workouts. They stress many different muscle groups, increase range of motion, and prepare you to run faster in races. When it comes to speed work, less is more.

# 1

# Interval Training

INTERVAL TRAINING IS the oldest, most studied, and most proven of all performance-boosting training methods for endurance athletes. First you get in shape, then you use intervals to get faster. Intervals were invented for middle-distance and distance track runners, where they worked so well that they soon spread to other sports like swimming and rowing.

Intervals can improve your race times in dramatic fashion, but also require a balanced, judicious approach. Too much interval training leads to burnout and slower races. I often tell runners they should consider that intervals carry a warning label: 'Handle with care.'

Interval training was born in Germany in the late 1930s when a coach-physiologist named Woldemar Gerschler teamed up with a cardiologist named Herbert Reindel to produce the first systematic training system. They based their programme on heart rates, and also on the four variables of track training: distance, speed, number of repetitions, and the rest interval between repetitions.

Today, most runners use 'interval' to describe the fast part of their workout. Originally, however, Gerschler and Reindel used it for the rest interval between repetitions. They considered this an essential ingredient in allowing for appropriate heart recovery between fast runs.

In 1939, a German runner, Rudolf Harbig, coached by Gerschler and Reindel, smashed the 800-meter world record by a huge margin,

1.6 seconds. When the interval-trained Emil Zatopek won the 5,000 metres, 10,000 metres, and marathon at the 1952 Olympic Games, the interval-training method gained even stronger footing.

Today, the effectiveness of interval training is universally accepted, although not universally adored. When I was in high school in the mid-1960s, all coaches wanted their athletes to mimic Jim Ryun's heavy interval programme. However, I despised intervals on the track, and felt that the workouts made me weaker, not stronger. I responded much better to LSD training (long slow distance).

Years later, I learned how to do interval workouts appropriate to my ability and goals. I've continued ever since. Interval training produces great results. You just have to learn how to apply it. And also to stop after six to eight weeks before you get burned out.

**Run classic intervals:** According to modern interpretation, confirmed by many studies, the most effective time and pace for interval training is 4 to 5 minutes at close to your VO2 max pace. In other words, this is the workout that will give you the biggest boost. You don't need to be treadmill-tested in a lab to find your VO2 max pace. It's essentially the same as your two-mile race pace.

With that information, you can put together a classic interval workout with several repetitions of 800 metres to 1,200 metres (4 to 5 minutes) at your two-mile pace. Remember: Don't overdo it. This isn't the kind of workout you do every day, and faster isn't better. I recommend repeating this workout no more than once a week for four to six weeks.

**Run intervals of different lengths:** The best way to avoid staleness and burnout from interval training is to run a variety of quite-different interval workouts. For example, you could run 3,200s one week and 200s the next week. In the first case, you'd do just a couple of repeats at a pace considerably slower than the above classic workout. In fact, you might run at your half-marathon pace rather than your two-mile pace.

The next week, you could switch to six to eight 200s at a considerably faster pace – roughly your one-mile race pace. That's the beauty of intervals – you can use them to hone every part of your running fitness, from your endurance to your final sprint. When combined with a one- or two-mile warm-up, and a similar cool-down, intervals make a complete workout.

**To peak, run fewer, shorter, faster intervals:** When top runners want to peak for their best races of the year, they begin to 'periodise' their interval training. In other words, they decrease their total running to increase recovery and freshness while also doing shorter, faster intervals. The goal is to rest, build strength, and build speed simultaneously. Each part of the programme reinforces the others. With intervals, you can turn this into a science.

When you're approaching top fitness, it's sometimes smarter to skip a workout than to nail it. Young runners often can't appreciate this approach. Veterans understand it through their rearview mirror. 'When you're peaking, a day off can be better than a workout,' says Meb Keflezighi. 'We need to be less a Type A personality.'

## 2

# The Fartlek System

FOR A RIGOROUS, almost mathematically precise training plan, you can't beat interval training. For similar results with a lot more fun and spontaneity, fartlek training offers a great alternative.

Fartlek was developed in the mid-1930s by a Swedish coach named Gosta Holmer. The word always provokes a giggle from English speakers. Translated from the original Swedish, it means 'speed play'.

The 'play' aspect of fartlek running is what separates it from other training methods. To be clear, this isn't the type of play enjoyed by three-year-olds splashing with rubber duckies in a bathtub. There's no free lunch in running. No training programme produces results without serious dedication and application, not to mention lots of sweat.

Instead, with fartlek training, you run as hard as you want for as long (or as short) as you want, and only when you feel like it. Then you slow down or walk until you feel like going at it again. This is very different from interval training, where workouts are planned before you start running, and there's a prescribed distance and time for everything.

The great Scandinavian runners conducted their fartlek workouts on soft, undulating pine-forest trails. They might begin one fast burst at the foot of a hill, or at the large boulder where the trail curved. The burst would continue until the runner felt it was time to stop. The distance didn't matter, the time didn't matter. The Swedes ran according to spontaneous effort, and felt that the pristine natural surroundings assisted their quest.

When Gunder Hagg and Arne Andersson set six world records for the 1-mile in the early 1940s, the value of Swedish fartlek training was demonstrated. Soon, athletes from Great Britain, Australia, New Zealand, and other British Commonwealth countries began to follow the fartlek programme. They believed the free, undisciplined approach meshed well with the human spirit, while also connecting runners to trails, forests, and the natural environment. Man and Nature combined. Who could improve upon it?

The beauty of fartlek running is its flexibility. You run slow and fast, slow and fast, as your soul and motivation direct you. While a Swedish pine-needle forest can't be beat as a training locale, you can also do fartlek on a long, straight road.

In this way, fartlek becomes interval training, only without the stopwatch and clipboard. Fartlek is unscripted speed work, and capable of producing significant results. It remains one of the world's favourite and most-proven training systems.

**Use the whole environment:** Interval training is done on a flat, fast track. Fartlek training takes place in the real world, full of all its warts, wobbles, and natural landmarks. Run uphills, downhills, and sprints to the tree with the recently-broken limb. Recover for 30 seconds, 3 minutes, or even 10 minutes. Go as you please. No two workouts could or should ever be the same.

**Run short, run long:** The best fartlek workouts are also the most varied. Run some surges quite short and fast – much faster than you would normally run in 5K races, for example. Go longer on other surges, and use another pace, say your half-marathon or marathon pace.

You don't have to alternate short and long in a specific formula. Mix them together however you want, or do a few more short bursts one day of the week, and a few more long pickups on another day. Don't strive to do the same fartlek routine as the week before, so you can compare total time. Throw comparisons out the window.

**Go green:** I have actually done fartlek training on the side of long, straight roads, as mentioned earlier. When circumstances force me to run alongside roads, this is how I make workouts more tolerable. But parklands are much more inspiring. I recommend you do fartlek workouts in your favourite green space. Treat yourself – it's worth it.

I have noticed that fartlek running includes so much inherent variety that I can enjoy multiple laps of the same looping path. Normally, I never do this. I get bored much too soon. But when I do a fartlek session in my favourite local park, I normally retrace the same 1.5-mile loop four times.

It just happens to be the best, grassiest, smoothest, most rolling loop in the vicinity. Despite the repetitions, I find that time passes quickly, because I am doing different fartlek bursts at different parts of each loop.

# 3

# Races as Training

WHEN RUNNERS THINK about getting faster, they generally focus on their training efforts – ways to get faster through specific workouts and a general uptick in training intensity. But there's another, completely different path. Don't worry about your training. In fact, keep it just the same – mostly quite easy. Simply add more races to your schedule.

I did this all through college, the years when I ran my best and fastest, from 8:45 in the two-mile to 2:14:29 in the marathon. I performed nearly 90 percent of my training at a comfortable, relaxed pace. In this way, I managed to keep my aerobic fitness and endurance at a very high level.

At the same time, my college's regular schedule of dual meets and invitational events forced me to race often. This was my speed work. While I lost almost all my track races – outkicked at the end – the regular competition built my speed and efficiency.

During any given track season, I might improve my mile time from 4:25 to 4:20, a small difference. More importantly, my 10-mile race pace dropped by a similar 5 seconds per mile for a total gain of 50 seconds. Those 50 seconds brought me many road victories over runners who beat me on the track. They couldn't match my endurance strength over longer distances. The gains wouldn't have happened without my frequent 1-mile and 2-mile efforts.

After college, my road performances deteriorated. At first, I didn't understand why. Before long, however, I realised that I had lost the zip that comes from track racing. To regain the lost speed, I began doing intervals, fartlek, tempo runs, and hill training.

I also started entering more road races. I used most of these as workouts, not to chase victories or personal bests. The goal was always to race myself into top shape, as I had in college. A word of caution here: Don't combine frequent racing with regular speed work between your races. Pick one or the other.

**Enter 5K races as speed work:** The 5K distance is the most popular race distance in the country, meaning that you can often find one close to home. By including 5Ks in your training, you'll not only get faster at the 3.1-mile event, but also improve your efficiency at longer distances. This could end up helping you trim minutes off your half-marathon best, and even more off your marathon PB.

Races provide a benefit difficult to obtain through workouts. They 'harden' you like tempered steel to high, sustained exertions. They teach you how to extend your limits beyond what you imagined possible.

**Use 5K races as interval workouts:** I often enter 5K races where my goal isn't a fast finish time, but a solid workout within the race. For example, I like to test myself by running hard for a mile, floating the middle mile to get some recovery, and then running hard the last mile.

I have developed more than one way to run these interval 5Ks. Sometimes, I'll hold back a bit for the first 2.1 miles, and then see how quickly I can cover the last mile. The goal here is to probe for my 5K red line.

I stay under it for the first two-thirds of the distance, and then push past it in the last third. This gives me a sense of pace-control that I can use in future races. It gets the body accustomed to race-pace effort.

**Run longer races as tempo workouts:** I enjoy entering races for the wonderful social occasions they represent – a chance to catch up with many friends. But I don't always feel like making a max effort over the full race distance. I save those go-for-the-gold attempts for just one or two races per season.

Half-marathons have become so popular that they are among the biggest, most enjoyable of races. Rather than going full tilt for 13.1 miles, I often break up a half-marathon into several tempo runs. I might run my half-marathon goal pace (roughly tempo-run pace) for miles 3 to 6, and miles 9 to 12.

The other miles, I go steady but relaxed. This approach gives me practice and confidence at my goal pace without overly fatiguing me. Also, I only need one easy day before and after such an effort. This allows me to continue focusing on key workouts for my biggest upcoming race.

# 4

# Hill Training for Speed

HILL TRAINING PROVIDES more strength and speed stimulus than any other form of training. No wonder flat-landers from states like Florida seek out highway overpasses, stadium stairs, parking garages, and even the stairways in tall office buildings. Meanwhile, those who live in hilly areas – like the Rift Valley in Kenya, the Rocky Mountains, the rollers of Western Pennsylvania, and the ski slopes of Vermont, and many other regions – gain vast benefits because they don't have much choice.

I was lucky enough to grow up in a coastal region with relatively flat running near the ocean and local rivers, but plenty of steep hills heading inland. I could run mostly flat, mostly up and down hills, or combine the two. I didn't think of it as Nirvana fifty years ago. I do now.

From the beginning, I took readily to hill running. I have a short shuffling stride that seems well tuned to hills. I could just shift down into a low gear, almost like driving a car, and motor my way upward. I caught and passed other runners on the hills – that gave me a positive attitude.

I also learned to visualise each and every hill as a distinct quest – one with a beginning, middle, and end. I enjoyed tackling these challenges, and feeling triumphant when I got to the top. Completing a hill feels like an achievement to me. It counts for more than just passing another mile marker.

In my first Boston Marathon, I reached the top of Heartbreak Hill without even realising it. After years of reading about Heartbreak, I had assumed it would rival Mount Everest. It turned out Heartbreak wasn't as bad as several hills I ran regularly on my training routes. Hills are often more of a mental obstacle than a physical one.

A few years later, I learned how New Zealand's Arthur Lydiard produced Olympic champions with hill-repeat sessions. This was new to me. I had previously simply run courses that included tough hills here and there. Now I selected a particular hill, and ran up and down it many times for a highly effective strength and speed workout.

**Focus on form:** Efficient hill running demands good form. Any amount of wasted effort gets multiplied when you're churning uphill. Run with a short, slightly choppy stride, and likewise keep your arm motion quick and compact.

Focus your eyes on the ground 10 to 15 yards in front of you. Yes, you'll be tempted to look up toward the top of the hill. But do this only once or twice. The remaining distance might psych you out, and the head movement will yank you away from your most economical form.

**Run by effort, not pace:** No one can maintain their flat-land pace on uphills. Don't even try. Rather, concentrate on effort. Keep your breathing rate and volume exactly the same as what you were doing on the flats. Aim for *even-effort* running.

Don't panic if you suddenly realise that you're overdoing it. Relax, and slow down just slightly to get back into equilibrium.

I'm no fan of corny mantras like 'I love the hills, and the hills love me.' Who can believe this in the middle of a killer race? That said, I think a little reassuring self-talk is appropriate on hills. I prefer: 'I know how to stay relaxed and maintain effort on hills, so I can run strong to the finish.' It's wordier, but more doable.

**Give hill repeats a try:** This is what I learned from Arthur Lydiard.

Almost anywhere you might live, you can find a clear, smooth, traffic-free hill that's perfect for hill repeats. Try to locate one that's 100 to 300 yards long. Run repeats up and down it a number of times. This is the optimal way to get a great hill workout.

You can run different distances and efforts on hills, just as on the track. I tend to follow a basic hill-repeat pattern about 75 percent of the time. I like to run 30 to 40 seconds uphill at something between my one-mile and 5K race effort. At the end of each, I walk or jog slowly back to my start point, being careful to avoid excessive pounding on my legs. I usually start with four repeats at the beginning of a training build-up, and increase to ten. With several miles for warm-up and cool-down, this makes a complete workout.

# 5

# Downhill Training

IN ALL MY years reading about runners and running, I've only encountered one or two articles about downhill training. This strikes me as very odd, because I consider it one of the best ways to get smoother and faster. It has worked well for me on many occasions.

To appreciate why, you must understand a much-overlooked fact about running. When we run, we fall from one foot to the next. This doesn't happen with walking. Walkers skim along the road surface. When they put their front foot to the ground, it is straight. It has no bend to it.

Runners hop from foot to foot, bending their knees to absorb the impact of each stride, and then launching into the next stride. We spend about 60 percent of the time in flight, with both feet off the ground. After flying a modest distance through the air, we fall back to the ground.

The falling and bending allows us to develop maximum muscle power and tendon elasticity. These propel us upward and forward. They also make running a more efficient form of movement than walking at speeds above 4-½ miles per hour. If you don't believe me, try walking a mile at 12-minute pace someday. Running 12-minute pace is far easier.

Downhills add stress to your running because the down slope lengthens your stride, boosts your speed, and increases the vertical drop from one footfall to the next. Each time your front foot crashes back to the ground, you hit with two to three times more force than you would on the flat. Physiologists note that downhill running causes 'eccentric' muscle contractions to cushion the force.

There's good and bad to this. The bad is pain and soreness. The morning after the downhill Boston Marathon, the city is filled with runners walking backwards as they descend stairways. Their quadriceps muscles have been trashed by too many eccentric contractions over the 26-mile trek.

The good is obviously that you can run faster on downhills. Also, through regular training on downhills, you can develop a smoother and faster running style. You'll learn one of running's most important skills – how to stay relaxed, instead of tensing up, as your speed increases. Many studies have also shown that such training diminishes the soreness from subsequent eccentric running and hard races.

**Start on a short, modest slope:** I always suggest that runners interested in downhill training begin on a smooth, grassy hill. The soft turf underneath will cushion your footfalls. Look for a hill that's at least 70 to 80 yards long with a modest slope. Avoid steep downhills. Run down this hill at about your one-mile race effort. Pick up speed gradually and decelerate gradually. Nothing abrupt. Don't sprint or attempt to reach top speed. Concentrate on moving as smoothly and relaxed as you can.

Stay controlled, and let yourself flow downward with the slope. At your first downhill workout, do no more than four or five such accelerations. Walk and jog slowly back to your beginning point. If you don't have access to a grassy downhill, pick a smooth asphalt road with even less down slope.

**Make haste slowly:** For the next four to six weeks, do a similar workout, adding just one or two more downhill accelerations per week. You'll feel that you could do more. After all, downhill running is easier than flat and uphill running.

Except that it's not easy on your joints and muscles. So proceed cautiously. If you develop any unusual aches or pains, lay off the downhills until you are completely recovered.

**Use efficient form:** As you might imagine, optimal downhill running form is quite different from uphill form. First, don't pump with your arms. The down slope and gravity will supply all the power you need.

Instead, calm your arms, and use them mainly to balance your upper body. Don't let them swing crazily back and forth. That's wasted energy and momentum. You want to flow like a hoop rolling downward.

Don't lift, reach, or extend with your legs. Unnecessary work. You'll go plenty fast enough simply by 'becoming one' with the slope. I use this mantra: 'Put it down. Put it down. Put it down.' I'm referring to my front foot. Rather than trying to lengthen my stride, I put my front foot down as soon as possible. This trick leads to fast, flowing speed on downhills. I just coast along on the ride.

# 6

# The 30-20-10 Workout

THE RUNNING WORLD is full of coaches, trainers, and elite athletes who claim to have discovered special workouts of great value. We read about them all the time – in books, magazines, and lengthy internet articles. Often they feature runners who have won Olympic gold medals or set world records after using the recommended workout. That's great.

The problem is, none of these workouts have been proven to work for other runners. They definitely have not been tested on hundreds of less-Olympian runners. No one has conducted scientific experiments with A versus B comparisons of the much-heralded training session.

Yes, a 60-minute run is no doubt an excellent workout. But we have no way of knowing if 40 minutes of faster-paced running would be even better. The appropriate scientific trials haven't been conducted.

So we lurch forward in the pursuit of best workouts and training systems. We're rarely sure if a given approach will work for the many, or only for the few who have already prospered with it.

That's why I was so impressed several years ago when I read about a training experiment carried out in Denmark. The researchers actually performed an A versus B comparison, with striking results that introduced a simple, compelling new workout.

**Here's what happened:** The study team talked ten experienced runners into trying something different. Meanwhile, eight other subjects continued their normal routine – about 18 miles a week of steady training.

The ten guinea pigs had been doing much the same, but now reduced their weekly training distance by 50 percent. Their new programme dictated a highly specific workout pattern we can express as 30-20-10. They jogged for 30 seconds, ran somewhat faster for 20 seconds, and then sprinted the last 10 seconds of every minute.

They repeated this process four more times (to reach 5 minutes of running), jogged for 2 minutes of recovery (reaching 7 minutes), and completed the whole cycle twice more (for a grand total of 21 minutes of running). They did this workout three times a week. It may sound complicated the first time you read about it. But once you grasp the component parts, almost nothing could be simpler.

And the results? The Danish scientists tested both groups of runners before and after seven weeks of training. The 'control' subjects who continued their normal training ran essentially the same times in the one-mile and 5K before and after. The 'experimental' group, on the other hand, ran faster by 21 seconds in the 1-mile and 48 seconds in the 5K. This came after seven weeks of 30-20-10 training.

Not only that. The new workouts also had a beneficial effect on key health markers like blood pressure and low-density lipoproteins (LDL, the 'bad' cholesterol). You couldn't ask for much more: a workout that makes you both faster and healthier. Bring it on.

**Follow the basic script:** Since the 30-20-10 workout is simple and proven, I recommend trying it first just as it was created. But not three times a week. That was good for a science experiment, but you'll do better running it just once or twice a week for about a month. Then test yourself with a 5K race.

If you like the results, you can make 30-20-10 workouts a regular part of your training diet. Use the workout when you want to increase your speed. Don't do it too often or for too many weeks in a row. You're not aiming for journal publication. You're just trying to get faster. Less is better.

**Keep it fast:** The 'special sauce' in the 30-20-10 workout is the 10 seconds of sprinting at the end of each minute. That's what makes it different from many other workouts. So don't change this.

You might be tempted to try other similar patterns – perhaps 60-40-20. And that might be an outstanding workout. But who knows? It hasn't been tested. It's possible the longer durations would actually detract from inherent physiologic functions (muscular and cardiac) that make 30-20-10 so effective. So stick with the tried-and-true formula.

**Relax to the max:** Because the 30-20-10 workout is built on gradual acceleration, it allows you to practise continuous relaxation. While changing speeds, concentrate on retaining the easy rhythm you felt while jogging for the first 30 seconds. Move your legs faster when sprinting for 10 seconds, but keep all other body parts – face, shoulders, arms – as relaxed as possible.

# 7

# Run-Walk for Speed

THE RUN-WALK system keeps popping up in this book. That's because I consider it such an essential, fundamental, and adaptable training tool. It's tough to beat for beginning runners, those returning to running (or returning after injuries), or those increasing their miles to run a half-marathon or marathon. I have used it for all of these.

Now that I've turned the corner past seventy, I do more run-walk training and racing than ever before. I'm constantly amazed at the power and utility of run-walk. Indeed, I believe it holds the key to lifelong health through running – the ultimate goal of this book.

However, one thing I never expected was the way I would use run-walk for speed workouts. In recent years, I've done much of my summer speed training with the run-walk system, and enjoyed it more than I ever could have imagined. Indeed, it feels playful, the way a child runs and walks. It's also the way elite runners train. Only they call it intervals.

My run-walk speed training generally takes this form: Run, run faster, then walk. This is similar to the just-covered 30-20-10 workout, except that it uses walking for recovery rather than slow jogging. The walks provide an extra mental and physical boost. It's easy to run hard on your fast segments when you know they'll be followed by a walk.

I also use run-walk for longer workouts than 30-20-10, which, as

I noted, is primarily for high-end speed. I do run-walk training at everything from mile pace, to tempo pace, to marathon pace.

I have found that run-walk speed training works great on the roads, our most common training environment. Much as I love trails and parks, there aren't any adjacent to my home. Since I run in part to avoid our car-centric culture, I don't like driving even 5 minutes to a park. With run-walk speed, I can stroll down the driveway, turn onto the nearby roads, and begin my speed workouts.

**Run 2 minutes, walk 1 minute:** My favourite run-walk speed session begins with a mile or two warm-up consisting of slow running or relaxed run-walking. Then I switch to this pattern for the next several miles: Run 2 minutes, walk 1 minute. You might be tempted to point out that I haven't done anything fast yet.

But in practice, I do. I run the last 30 seconds of the two-minute segment fast. That is, I run the first 2 minutes as 90-30, with the 30 at about my 5K race pace. You could call it 90-30-60. It's all the same, just minutes versus seconds.

At my current fitness, I cover about one-third of a mile in a 3-minute segment. I'll do six to ten of these during a run-walk speed workout. If I add another mile or two of cool-down, that gives me a total run distance of 5 to 7 miles – pretty decent.

**Run 60 seconds, walk 30 seconds:** The great thing about run-walk training is that everyone has their own favourite ratio. My wife, who completed sixteen marathons in her twenties and thirties, now refuses to do any running that is not a run-walk. Why? Because she's a few years older than she once was, and hence a few strides slower. As a result, a continuous run feels slow and boggy to her.

She much prefers feeling light and fast. Who wouldn't? She achieves what she's looking for with a 60-30 run-walk. During her 60-second runs, she goes much faster than she would on a continuous 30- to 40-minute run.

That's a good thing on several fronts. It probably gives her a better overall cardiovascular workout. And she definitely enjoys it more. She finds it motivating, not depressing. Do what works best for you.

**Run 4 minutes, walk 1 minute:** I have used this workout to sharpen my marathon pace for the last several Boston Marathons. Let's say I'm running a 16-miler. I'll do the first 8 miles at a slow, steady running pace of about 10 minutes per mile.

Then I'll switch to a 4-1 run-walk for the last 8 miles. Once I've switched over, I run the 4-minute segments at about a 9-minute pace, while recovering with 1-minute walks.

I get the best of both worlds this way: endurance building, and running at slightly faster than my goal marathon pace. This programme has proven its value. It has gotten me to five straight Boston Marathon finishes.

# 8

# The Pre-Race Taper

FOR ANYONE WHO races, the taper is the most important part of the training programme. A taper is the days and sometimes weeks before a race when you decrease your training to increase your strength and freshness on race day. This is the season to ease back and harvest the fruits of your labour. Don't miscalculate. In particular, don't over-train during your taper. When this happens, you risk wasting your weeks and months of focused training.

When you begin to train harder, two things happen simultaneously. First, your potential for improved performance rises. Training is an investment in your future. However, in real time, your fatigue also increases, so the two tend to cancel each other out. In other words, you can't race your best when you are also training to the max.

Coaches and athletes have long understood this, of course. So they had to come up with a solution. Before their most important races, top athletes 'taper' (reduce) their training. This allows them to erase the fatigue, and to peak for a best-possible performance.

Peaking is so crucial to athletic success that it has been extensively studied. Fortunately, most of the studies have reached the same or very similar conclusions. The path to primo peaking is clear: Reduce your total training, but maintain (or even slightly increase) the speed of several workouts per week. Run less, run faster, and race your best on the chosen day.

A meta-analysis of twenty-seven tapering studies published

in *Medicine & Science in Sport & Exercise* reached the following conclusion: 'The optimal strategy is a two-week taper' with training volume reduced by 41 to 60 percent, 'while training frequency and intensity remain the same.' In other words, you should continue running the same number of days per week, but shorten each workout by up to 60 percent. Maintain the pace of your (shortened) speed runs.

You might think tapering would be great fun, with its decreased training load. However, most runners underestimate the emotional challenge. Don't be surprised if your knees begin creaking, your stomach sours, and you can't stop thinking that your training has been all wrong.

If disaster seems imminent, that's a good sign. It's perfectly normal. Don't panic. 'Race day magic' will make everything turn out fine on your big day.

**The one-week taper:** Most races of 5K or 10K only require a one-week taper. If the race is on Saturday or Sunday, just follow your normal days of running, but keep them short. If you typically run 4 miles at a time, run only 2 or 3 miles. During these short runs, do several surges at your goal race pace. You want your body to remember this pace, and to 'dial in' on it.

**The two-week taper:** This is the taper to follow if you are getting ready for a half-marathon. Two weeks before the half, run 10 to 12 miles at a comfortable pace. The week before, run 6 to 8 miles. Maintain the same frequency of runs during the week (three a week, four a week, etc) but run only 67 percent of your normal distance during the two-weeks-to-go period, and only 50 percent in the final week. As with other tapers, be sure to do some short speed sessions at your goal pace.

**The three-week taper:** Most recreational marathoners use a three-week taper. They need it, because they have increased their training quite dramatically in the previous three, four, or more months of dedicated marathon training.

The marathon also demands a longer taper because the distance is great enough to require full glycogen storage, muscle freshness, proper hydration, and complete mental focus. You've got to train to the max for a great marathon, but then you also have to taper to the max.

Three weeks before the marathon, you can complete a long run of 12 to 16 miles at a steady, comfortable pace. Two weeks before, reduce your long-run distance to 8 to 12. One week before, run 6 to 10 miles for your long run. Continue with the same number of your other, shorter weekly runs, but decrease the distance of each. They might drop from 8 to 6 to 4 miles apiece.

At least once a week, do several miles at your normal tempo-run pace, and maybe finish with three or four strides for relaxed, faster running. The faster runs will lift your knees and your spirits. You'll need both on marathon race day.

# 9

# Tempo Training

ALL RUNNERS REALISE there are different shades of speed. Take Usain Bolt, for instance. Tall, muscular, and long-legged, he's an almost literal 'Lightning Bolt'. No one has ever run as fast as Bolt, or collected more Olympic gold medals in the sprints. He's one of a kind. So is his speed.

We recreational runners know we aren't lightning bolts. Yet many of us could actually beat Usain Bolt in a 5K road race. That's because there's one thing called sprint speed, and quite another called endurance speed. At one level, these depend on the muscle fibres you were born with. On another level, they develop from your training.

Tempo training has become one of the most popular and valued forms of runner training, because it's designed to increase endurance speed. It helps you maintain a strong pace for longer. That's job one for just about all road runners, whether we're preparing for a 5K or a marathon. We want to run a handful of seconds faster per mile, and then to maintain that pace for as long as possible.

Training at tempo pace helps us accomplish this. Tempo pace rests midway between the easy, relaxed pace of everyday runs, and the high-intensity effort demanded by intervals. When the famous American coach and physiologist, Jack Daniels, PhD, discovered tempo training while living in Scandinavia, he learned that tempo runs should last about 20 minutes.

Daniels and others have evolved the classic tempo run modestly through the years. But only modestly. Beware of so-called tempo runs that last 10 or 12 miles, or even longer. That's not a tempo run. It might be a great workout, but I believe many runners over-train by extending tempo runs longer than the original 20 minutes.

Tempo runs are almost universally described as 'hard but controlled'. If that's too vague for you, run your tempo efforts at your 10-mile race pace – a little slower than 10K pace, a little faster than half-marathon pace. Physiologically speaking, tempo runs raise your lactate threshold, so you can run longer at this pace before your muscles shut down from too much lactic acid.

In early 2017, Andrew Vickers, a runner and cancer statistician, published research that gave an important boost to tempo training. Vickers asked several thousand runners what kind of training they did prior to their best races. He expected tempo training to be associated with improved half-marathon and marathon performance, and it was.

He was surprised to discover that the runners also reported tempo training improved their 5K and 10K races. Its effectiveness covered essentially the whole racing spectrum. That's why so many runners use tempo runs in their training.

**Run hard but controlled for 20 minutes:** In this classic take on a tempo run, you begin with several easy warm-up miles, and then run hard for 20 minutes. Once you settle into your pace, relax as much as possible. The goal is to get your body accustomed to holding this rhythm without straining at it.

You shouldn't be exhausted at the end. You should feel a pleasant sort of fatigue, but no more. Most runners feel completely recovered the day after a tempo run. In fact, some pack a tempo run and interval workout into back-to-back sessions on successive days.

**Don't run too fast or too far:** Many runners suffer from a case of 'more must be better' disease. This trap is easy to fall into when doing tempo runs, because the pace doesn't demand near-all-out effort, as intervals do. Tempo runs fall into the category of sub-max running – slower than your best.

That means you could quite easily go faster and/or farther. Resist the temptation. Settle into comfortably hard, then switch to auto pilot. If you went faster or farther, you'd be almost racing, which produces an exhaustive effect opposite to what you want from tempo training.

**Try cruise intervals:** As part of his thorough investigations into tempo training, coach Jack Daniels devised a workout he calls 'cruise intervals'. These are 6- to 8-minute runs at tempo pace, with brief jogs between them.

For example, you might run three times 8 minutes, with a mere 60-second jog between the repeats. This is just another way – a mental variation, really – to achieve the same end result as a tempo workout. Some runners find cruise intervals easier, some simply appreciate having several options.

# 10

# Out-and-Back Speed

BY NOW, YOU will have noted several of the main themes that weave through this book. They include: Simple is often best. Running is a low-tech sport. You don't improve your fitness and performance with digital devices, diet 'breakthroughs' that usually aren't, or a closet full of the newest gear.

I've always gotten better results from KISS: Keep It Simple, Stupid.

When it comes to strong, measurable road workouts, one of the most useful running routes is the out-and-back course. You start where you are, and run to the postbox. Or the one-mile mark. Or whatever other goal you have set for yourself. Then you turn around, and run back to your start point.

I have long used a series of out-and-back road courses to enhance my toughness and performance. Specifically, I cover the same course three weeks in a row. I run from Point A to Point B, and then turn around for the return to Point A. Each week, I try to run a little faster on the return trip from Point B to Point A.

Most runners I know don't like out-and-back courses. We tend to choose running routes that trace a circular or quadrangular path back to the starting point. We like new vistas. We don't like retracing our steps.

But out-and-back courses have many advantages. They give security and confidence to beginning runners who crave familiar, close-to-home courses. When you are increasing distance, they make it easy to add small chunks at a time. You just run a few more blocks before turning around.

Best of all, at least in my view, they offer a simple-yet-excellent way to improve your pace. Here's how I do it. I begin with a long, relaxed warm-up of 2 to 4 miles to my selected turnaround point. I don't time the first half of my run. It's not really important.

I concentrate on reaching the turnaround feeling loose and comfortable. Then, on the return, I start running harder. Now I time myself. The goal is to complete this run three weeks in a row, always with a faster return trip.

**Start slow, finish faster:** When doing out-and-back speed, job one is keeping the first half of your run slow. Don't feel guilty about it. The warm-up is a key part of the run. It provides the foundation for all that follows. You have to go slow enough that you can run quite a bit faster on your return. That's job two.

**Return fast, faster, and faster-yet:** When I do my first out-and-back in a series, I know that two more will follow. I also know that I'll try to run the three return legs in a sequence of increasing effort. That is, I'll aim for: hard, harder, and harder still. With this in mind, I can mentally gauge the efforts that are required.

On week one, I'll run comfortably fast – at a controlled tempo pace. I should finish tired but invigorated. On week two, I'll kick it up a notch, but not so much that I'm gasping for breath at the end. On week three, I dig deeper. I don't run race pace – not quite – but I push to about a 90- to 95-percent effort.

The week-two and week-three runs are the ones that produce big fitness pay-offs. But the first is also important. It gets the ball rolling.

**Keep track of time:** I always time the return run closely. I want to be able to see that my increasing efforts produce a positive outcome. That builds confidence. The out-and-back speed run trains both body and mind.

The body feels the increased effort coming back, and adapts over the several weeks. The mind registers the improvement on my watch. It accepts that something even better and faster is possible if I should decide to race soon. Seeing is believing.

I can't give you a precise formula for the three faster return runs. Each of us, and each of our course distances and topographies, is too variable for that. But here's a guideline for the second 3 miles of a 6-mile out-and-back speed run. Run marathon effort or slightly faster on week one, half-marathon effort on week two, and 10K effort on week three.

# 11

# Speed Variety and the Magic of Three

IMPROVEMENT IN RUNNING never follows a linear upward path. Don't look for or expect straight lines. Instead, improvement goes up and down in peaks and valleys. The goal isn't to avoid the valleys, which are inevitable, and also highly valuable when you have planned for them. Rather, you want your peaks to keep getting higher.

To achieve this, you must vary your training in at least two ways. You need to switch up the types of workouts you are focusing on, and the durations (lengths of time) you do each.

I first recognised how these two function together while covering races for *Runner's World*. I would go to a major road race where one runner placed higher than expected. Naturally, I asked him or her what caused the big improvement. 'I just changed to a new coach,' the runner would say. 'The results are amazing. I can't wait to see what I'll be running in six months.'

Six months later, I'd see the same runner at another big race. Only this time he or she finished far down the results list. The expected improvement didn't happen. I asked why. All I got in return was a shoulder shrug, and a long, sad face.

I decided to experiment on myself. I subjected myself to various training systems, as if I had just changed from one coach to a new one with a different workout programme. I tried long runs, hill sprints, interval 400s, tempo runs, and so forth. I did the specific hard workout – and no other hard workout – at least once a week, and monitored how I felt and performed.

No matter what workout I tried, I felt great for three weeks. On the fourth week, however, I could feel the air coming out of my tyres. Clearly, I was over-trained and headed in a bad direction.

That's when I developed the 'Magic of Three' strategy. It states that you should only do three weeks of a particular kind of hard workout. After three weeks, it's time to recover, and change things up.

**Do less (at times) to achieve more:** To improve, all runners need to gradually add more stress to their training. This is the way we apply Hans Selye's famous General Adaptation Syndrome. We train harder. We rest, recover, and adapt. And then we train harder again, beginning the next cycle.

Selye observed that without the rest and adaptation, the body gets weaker instead of stronger. The resulting crash used to be called 'overtraining'. Today physiologists use the term 'overreaching', which is wonderfully apt, but essentially the same. If you reach too high in your training, because you are always trying to do more, you will too soon hit a wall.

It's far smarter to plan regular recovery periods than to have them batter your training progress. In my experience, the recovery should come every fourth or fifth week. Keep running, but take a break from hard workouts. Go easy every day for a full week.

**Switch gears:** The Magic of Three system notes that there are many fantastic workouts. However, no single type of workout is superior to all others. All are capable of producing great results. The 'magic' comes from the way you weave workouts together.

Don't repeat any particular hard-day workout more than three weeks in a row. Then take a recovery week. The system produces optimal results if you change the focus of your key workout every month. Switch from hills to tempo runs to intervals. Try long runs and fartlek workouts. Include 30-20-10 workouts and out-and-back speed runs.

Whenever you begin to feel a little stale, stop the hard workouts you've been doing, and swap in something else. You'll notice both mental and physical benefits.

**Fitter, stronger, faster:** To reach your fitness and performance goals, you need to train hard. You need to train *consistently* hard. However, you can't train hard all the time, and you shouldn't try.

Instead, recognise that your fitness and performance follow an undulating slope. They curve up, and down, and up again. It's your job to bend your training to match these slopes. Because they will not bend to you. They will break you.

# SECTION 6

# RUNNING FOREVER

# A Day to Remember

I OFTEN NOTE that every marathon is full of unexpected surprises. No matter how many you have done previously, you can't expect your next marathon to unfold in a predictable manner. The distance is too great, the number of variables too large. You never know what awaits around the next corner, or in the next mile. It could be wonderful – a loud, rhythmic rock band, or a cheering fan in a delightful costume. It could be tragic.

The 2013 Boston Marathon held more surprise than any race I have ever run. I began in a completely cheerful mood on a gorgeous day. In fact, I felt quite special to be running Boston again on the 45th anniversary of my win in 1968. I was the oldest returning champion in the field. I confess to swelling with pride.

I also had great company on the road in the persons of John and Megan Valentine. John, a cancer doc from Vermont, was my oldest training partner. We had first run together in the early 1960s. Fifty years later, still fit but considerably slower, we still enjoyed each other's company. His daughter Megan was young, strong, and fast, not to mention a motormouth. She was our cheerleader. She kept up a steady stream of encouragement.

While we ran the course, my wife, brother, and kids drove the parallel roads, stopping every 5 miles or so. They carried large, colourful 'Go Amby' signs to the course-side, and greeted me with hugs and kisses. My sister, a below-the-knee amputee since childhood, was sitting in the finish-line stands, waiting to applaud my final strides.

By now I suspect you are remembering something about the 2013 Boston Marathon. Wasn't that the one with the bomb explosions at the end? Didn't several people die? Yes, and yes. But until the first bomb detonated at 2:49 p.m., Boston time, none of us had any reason to expect a tragedy.

Indeed, John, Megan, and I were enjoying a perfect run. We were hitting our planned pace, designed to get us to the finish in a time of 4:15. My brother, Gary, drove the family van through the congested Boston streets without incident. I saw everyone at all the appointed spots, and felt elevated by their support.

The more miles we put behind us, the better we felt. Framingham. Natick. The screaming girls of Wellesley College at the halfway point. Our marathon couldn't be going any better. We topped Heartbreak Hill in complete control at 21 miles, and soon started the long run down Beacon Street to Fenway Park.

There we passed the 25-mile marker. We knew every inch of the remaining course. First Kenmore Square. Then a turn onto Commonwealth Avenue before the famous 'right on Hereford, left on Boylston'. I started to get giddy. Who else in the race could say they had first run Boston forty-eight years earlier, and won the whole thing forty-five years ago?

Nothing could stop us now, not with only a mile remaining. At least nothing we had ever experienced before.

Suddenly I noticed a knot of runners in the road ahead. They didn't seem to be moving. Strange. When we got there a minute later, the knot had grown into a crowd. I could see a few police ahead, but no one knew why they had stopped us.

My cell phone rang. I had carried it this day for the first and only time in my running life. I figured I might need it to stay in touch with the family van.

'Hello,' I said.

'It's Cristina.' My wife. We are incapable of chatting without jokes and wisecracks.

'Hey, you'll never guess ...,' I began, planning to tell her about the weird blockade.

'Shut up,' she said. Words she had never directed to me before, nor since.

I had never heard such urgency in Cristina's voice, so I stopped talking, and listened.

'We're getting reports of a bomb explosion at the finish,' she said. '*Don't you dare keep running.* Get back to the hotel. I'll meet you there.'

Now I was shaking with a fear I didn't fully understand. Even though we were on Commonwealth Avenue only a mile from the finish, we had not heard nor seen any bombs. Several streets of brownstones and other taller commercial buildings blocked everything.

On our eight-block walk to the Sheraton Hotel, we saw dozens of sirens-blazing police, fire, and ambulance vehicles. The response was amazing. We watched in mute shock. There was nothing we could do.

Over the next hours and days, we absorbed the full horror of the situation – the two explosions, the deaths, the maimed, the non-stop manhunt, the great city shaking with terror, and then struggling to right itself. We heard President Obama give one of his finest speeches, including the words: 'We carry on. We race. We strive. We build and we work and we love and we raise our kids to do the same. And this time next year on the third Monday in April, the world will return to this great American city to run harder than ever and to cheer louder for the 118th Boston Marathon. Bet on it.'

I came back the next year with John, Megan, and many other friends. We had unfinished business to take care of. In fact, I have returned to run Boston every year since 2013.

In each, I have followed three new personal traditions. First, I run for the Martin Richard Foundation, wearing its shirt, and honouring Martin. He's the eight-year-old killed next to the finish line in 2013. Several months earlier, after the shootings at the Sandy Hook School in Newtown, Connecticut, he had painted a squiggly poster that pleaded: 'No more hurting people. Peace.'

I now run with a small business card that I hand out mostly to youngsters lining the course. They represent the next generation of Boston runners and spectators. My card says: 'Thank you Boston Marathon fans. Your cheers and constant support are what makes Boston the world's greatest marathon. Signed, Amby Burfoot. First Boston, 1965. Boston winner, 1968.'

Lastly, when I reach the finish line, I do not run triumphantly across it. Once I did. I sprinted across the finish as fast as my tired legs could carry me. Now that seems all wrong. Winning is out of the question, my time insignificant.

Now I am in no rush. I have nothing to prove. To arrive here, I have already covered 26 miles. So I stop to walk. I want to appreciate these precious moments. I want to celebrate life – mine and all others.

I stop at the point where the second bomb exploded in 2013. I slow to a walk, and glance skyward in silent prayer and thanksgiving, though I am not a conventionally religious person. I turn backward to applaud the runners streaming toward me.

I turn forward again, mere yards from the finish line, and keep walking. I note the spot where Martin Richard and family stood in 2013, so very, very close to the finish line. Life is so precious, and so fleeting. If only I could hold onto this moment forever – this reaching the glorious Boston Marathon finish line.

I know I can't. But I can walk across the finish slowly, appreciatively, with gratitude. I can retain the memory in my mind's eye. It will sustain me for another year, and perhaps longer.

1

# Don't Stop. Ever.

NOT LONG AGO, I was completing a *Runner's World* feature article about 'Lifetime Running', similar to the main topic of this book. I decided to do one last interview with Stanford arthritis expert Dr. James Fries. His 'Runners Study', published in the *Annals of Internal Medicine*, has produced the most compelling evidence I know about the benefits of lifetime running and fitness.

Fries's report showed that runners lived about seven years longer than a matched control group with equally good demographics and health insurance. Not only that, but the runners encountered common disabilities – like knee ailments and lower-back pain – ten to sixteen years later in life than the controls. There was no downside to lifetime running. It produced nothing but win-win outcomes.

As we were reviewing these points, Fries uttered several powerful sentences that I hadn't heard before. Or maybe I simply hadn't registered their import. 'Aging begins when we are in our twenties,' he told me. 'If you want to delay the aging process, that's the time to begin running.' Or any time before late life.

Fries continued: 'What you can't do is wait until you are seventy and then begin taking Geritol or some other elixir. The damage has been done, and you can't undo it. The runners in my study derived benefit from the cumulative effect of years and years of continuous exercise.'

In other words, life and running are not part-time sports. They demand full-time, across-the-decades attention.

The very next day I read an astonishing new paper published in the *Mayo Clinic Proceedings* (in early 2017). It followed almost 4,000 adults in their 60s and 70s. Some of the subjects in the journal study disregarded the obstacles they faced, and continued a regular exercise programme. They simply refused to quit. Others gave up and stopped. When the researchers compared the two groups, they found amazing differences.

Those who kept at it, despite two or more chronic conditions, enjoyed a 35 to 47 percent reduction in mortality compared to the non-exercisers with the same health issues. The authors concluded: 'Physical activity produced beneficial effects in all individuals with any specific chronic conditions.'

Running and other endurance exercise seems to prevent almost everything bad. Or as Mayo Clinic endurance expert Michael Joyner, MD, puts it: 'Regular exercise basically erases the effects of several serious conditions.'

**To every thing, there is a season:** I won the Boston Marathon in 1968 when I was 21 years old, and have been getting slower every day since then. At 70+, it now takes me almost twice as long to finish Boston. Or, for that matter, any run I undertake anywhere at any time. If I followed every piece of advice in this book's 'Gaining Speed' section, I would still be slower in five years. No one outruns aging.

But that's not the point. These days, I'm not trying to win the Boston Marathon. I'm happy to be alive, healthy, and vigorous. Moving forward still excites me, no matter what the pace. As long as I'm still moving … well, that means I'm alive and well. Which is a beautiful thing.

**Make your own rules:** My friend Dave McGillivray is race director of the Boston Marathon, and has finished Boston himself 45 years (and counting) in a row. Until a few years ago, he also used to run his age in miles on every birthday. He hit 60 miles on his 60th birthday.

I called Dave the next day to congratulate him, but also with a few words of wisdom. 'You can't keep running your age,' I said. 'Don't hold yourself to an impossible standard. Be flexible.'

The next year, Dave covered 61 miles. But this time he included a bit of swimming and a lot of bicycling. 'This is my game,' Dave explained to friends. 'I get to make the rules.' Proving he is as smart as he is fit and disciplined.

**Dare greatly:** In April, 1910, President Teddy Roosevelt gave one of his most famously rousing speeches to a large crowd at the Sorbonne in Paris. 'It is not the critic who counts,' Roosevelt said. 'The credit belongs to the man who is actually in the arena, whose face is marred by dust and sweat and blood.'

Roosevelt added that victory is never assured. 'At the least, he fails while daring greatly, so that his place shall never be with those cold and timid souls who know neither victory nor defeat.'

I agree. Dare greatly, but also intelligently. Make your own rules, then stick with them.

2

# The Hill-Running Elixir

IF YOU'VE FOLLOWED me to here on the *Run Forever* journey, the advice to run short, fast hills will likely surprise you. Most of this book, including even the 'Gaining Speed' section, contains adjectives like slow, controlled, moderate, and less-than-all-out. That's because most running should follow those guidelines.

Eventually, however, we need to discuss the difference between merely logging minutes or miles, and actually increasing cardiovascular fitness. The two can be quite different. For example, if you have a pedometer, and follow the popular 10,000 steps routine, you feel gratified every time your digital display flicks over to five digits by day's end. You've put in your steps, and hit your target.

That's obviously a good thing. On the other hand, it doesn't actually guarantee that you have improved your cardiovascular (CV) fitness, which is generally evaluated on a treadmill or exercise bicycle. Those tests require you to warm up, and then push as hard as you can for 10 to 15 minutes. The final result is called your maximal aerobic capacity, shortened to VO2 max in scientific notation.

Your VO2 max assesses your peak fitness. It's a biological measure of your body's heart and muscle function. Ten thousand steps (or 6 miles, or 60 minutes) all track a physical quantity that's only partially connected to your actual physiology. In fact, it's possible to walk casually for 10,000 steps a day while barely budging your CV fitness.

This matters because CV fitness trumps steps. Hundreds of long-term, epidemiological studies have shown that CV fitness is perhaps the ultimate determinant of your longevity and disease prevention. Steps are good, no doubt about it. But CV fitness is better, with its direct connection to a higher VO2 max.

And CV fitness is most enhanced by relatively short but intense exertions. Therefore, the best and healthiest lifetime running programmes have to incorporate some hard, heart-pumping effort. For this, it's tough to beat a solid hill workout.

**Go hard, stay soft:** There's a simple, biomechanics reason why I saved short, fast hills for this final section of *Run Forever*. When you run fast on the flat (such as a track), you produce powerful, rapid-fire strides that hit the track hard – Thump! Thump! Thump! This sends shock waves through your feet and ankles, up to your knees, and beyond, to your hips and back.

Some aches and soreness are almost inevitable, and the risk of injury rises. When you're young and reaching for the stars, the gamble is worth it. As you get older, the risk becomes much less tolerable, because the first rule of lifetime running is to minimise the threat of injury.

Uphill running – even hill sprints – dramatically reduce the impact shock of running, and hence the chance of injury. How? First, you're not moving as fast as you would on a track (or a downhill). Second, since the hill rises up to meet you, your body falls a lesser distance before your feet hit the ground. When you run uphill, you run soft, so you run healthy.

**Add hill speed gradually:** When doing short hill sprints, be sure to follow the rule of gradual progression. Start with just two or three sprints up a moderate hill. They should last only 6 to 15 seconds. When you're finished, walk slowly back to your beginning point, and a little beyond. That way you can jog to your start line before leaning into the next sprint.

Each week, add one or two additional sprints until you reach a total of ten. There's no need for more. Extend the length of your hill efforts to 20 to 30 seconds if you're feeling strong. Another alternative: Run longer repeats on a modest hill one week, and shorter repeats on a steeper hill the next week. You can't go wrong with the mix-and-match approach.

Run your sprints on a hill that has a smooth, unbroken surface, and little to no traffic. When you're pumping hard, with eyes down, you won't be in the best position to monitor nearby cars.

**Sure-fire strength and speed:** Regular hill running gets the job done. It makes you stronger and faster. Many-time national age-group champion Pete Magill always uses hill sprints in his own training, and in the programmes he develops for other runners. Why?

Because hill running targets all three types of muscle fibre, from slow twitch to fast twitch. Hill sprints build your ability to deliver more force with every stride. They enhance your CV fitness. They make you stronger and fitter for life.

# 3

# Lose Ten Pounds

RUNNERS ARE NOT immune to midlife weight gain. In fact, the National Runners Health Study has shown that most runners gain one-half to one-pound per year during their thirties, forties, and fifties. That's 50 percent less than the average weight gain of non-runners during the same period, but it still adds up. After thirty years, it could easily total twenty to thirty pounds.

The extra weight almost never does you any good. For one thing, it's associated with higher risks for all the chronic lifestyle illnesses from diabetes to heart disease. It's also linked to higher incidence of cancers, and osteoarthritis of the knees and hips. Finally, the added pounds make you slower by about 2 seconds per pound per mile.

Aging makes you slower, and the extra pounds make you slower. That's a double whammy. Who wouldn't want to avoid half of it – the weight-gain half that you can control?

There is a bit of a silver lining here. If you continue running despite any gained weight, you will have substantial health advantages over non exercisers of your identical weight. (Actually, percent body fat is the real enemy. But you know your own body. You know if you're getting fatter or not.)

The advantage phenomenon is called the 'fat but fit' effect. The conclusion comes from multiple large population studies that tracked subjects for many years. Those who were fat but fit, because they exercised regularly, lived longer than unfit subjects who actually weighed less. In other words, fitness limits many of the harms of fatness. So keep running, no matter what.

But don't settle for your current weight if you're carrying more body fat than you should. 'Lean and fit' beats 'fat but fit', so why not aim for your healthiest and fastest weight? 'It's definitely good to be as fit as possible, no matter what your body weight,' says Harvard nutrition and health expert Walter Willett, MD. 'But it's also optimum to be lean. It shouldn't be a question of one or the other.'

For the most part, losing weight depends on self-discipline. You're a runner, so you've got plenty. You simply need to apply it to your food-consumption habits. Eat less first, then move more as an added bonus.

**Small changes yield big results:** You don't lose weight by eliminating favourite but unhealthy foods from your diet. The cravings soon come back, and may very well overwhelm you. The more proven way to lose weight is to change habits. Change yourself.

There are many ways to do this. If you apply 15 minutes of self-control at the supermarket, you'll return home without that bag of cookies that tempts you every afternoon. If a particular restaurant serves a high-calorie meal you can't resist, meet your friends at a different location. Some studies have shown that you can lose weight simply by placing those tempting snack items in a difficult to reach place – the back of the fridge or pantry.

**Eat more protein at lunch:** Here's a trick that could help you lose weight by eating a bit more. It comes from Nancy Clark, RD, author of the *Sports Nutrition Guidebook*, a best-seller among runners for forty years. Like many nutritionists, Clark believes we often skimp on protein at breakfast and lunch. This leads to greater hunger later in the day.

Instead of buying a half-pound (eight ounces) of sliced turkey at the deli counter for your lunchtime sandwich, buy nine ounces, says Clark. At home, divide the nine ounces into three portions of three ounces each. Use all three ounces in your wholegrain sandwich. This lunch will provide substantially more protein than the one ounce of turkey that many put on their sandwiches.

**Watch those alcoholic drinks:** Many of us slip into drinking a little more as we get older, notes Liz Applegate, PhD, a longtime nutrition editor at *Runner's World*. Maybe the kids have left the nest, and dinnertime is no longer a frantic affair. You could enjoy a cocktail before dinner, and some wine with your meal.

Alcohol is not a calorie-free treat, however. Quite the opposite, at seven calories per gram, alcohol calories add up quickly. Applegate suggests switching to a glass of sparkling water before dinner. Eliminating one cocktail or glass of wine per evening could subtract 35,000 calories a year. That's 10 pounds right there.

4

# Adaptive Excellence

THE HUMAN RACE has been adapting through the evolutionary millennia, and the same happens during the relatively scant years of a single human life. Change is constant. And as we age through our eight to ten decades, we don't get taller, stronger, faster, smarter. Entropy pushes us in the other direction.

This doesn't mean, however, that we should give up, and toss our cards on the table. Sure, I'm older and slower than yesterday, and tomorrow's outlook isn't all that rosy. Yet I refuse to stop thriving, striving, and seeking new challenges. How else are we going to feed the spirit within to keep it from withering?

In my seventies, I need high (but realistic) goals more than at any other time of my life, and I continue to set them. Everyone else past fifty should do the same.

I call this process 'adaptive excellence'. I'll never again run as fast as I did in my 20s – or 30s, 40s, 50s, or 60s – but that doesn't mean I should stop trying. It doesn't mean I no longer have any dreams and aspirations. In fact, I've got more than enough to fill the next decade.

In his retirement, my father wanted nothing so much as a porch, a rocking chair, a glass of lemonade, and a sunset. I'm also a big fan of porches, rocking chairs, lemonades, and long views over the countryside or the endless waves. I'll happily spend a few evenings in a rocker.

But I want much more. I've pursued excellence in different fields

– family, running, editorial work – all my life. I can't see any reason to stop just because I've reached Social Security age. I want to keep climbing mountains, at least metaphorically, even if they aren't as high and steep as ones I've tackled in the past.

That's what I mean by adaptive excellence. At every age of life, we should pursue high-but-not-impossible standards. Don't sit, and don't stand still. Keep moving forward.

**Don't stop setting goals:** A good goal is the greatest motivator. Goals keep us honest and focused, and purposeful. All lifetime runners learn to adapt and adjust. You don't set your sights on a sub-2-hour half-marathon. Instead you aim for two half-marathon finishes per year – one in the spring, one in the autumn.

An optimistic outlook is key. Don't get depressed if you can't qualify for the Boston Marathon. Instead, commit to running 1,000 miles in the next 12 months. Track your progress scrupulously. Share it with friends on social media, or more privately. Tell them to hold you accountable, and to join the celebration when you reach your target.

**Try something new:** The endurance sports world has mushroomed so much in recent years, it's hard to imagine what they'll think up next. We've already got half-marathons, duathlons, triathlons, trail runs, mud runs, paint runs, zombie runs, relay runs, burro runs, nude runs, and midnight runs. Tomorrow and next year will no doubt bring more endurance innovation.

I'm not making fun of these events. I see them all as great opportunities. Pick one you've never done before, probably something you would have considered stupid a few years back. And give it a go.

**Run an annual race every year:** Most towns and cities have a big annual race these days, with both longer and shorter distances included among the options. If your town doesn't have one, there's almost certainly one within a reasonable driving distance. In November,

1963, I drove 50 miles with some friends to run the biggest race in my state, Connecticut. It's called the Manchester Road Race, held every year on Thanksgiving Day morning.

More than half a century later, I'm still running the same race every Thanksgiving. I've finished Manchester in blizzards, in heavy rain, with pneumonia, and with Achilles tendinitis so bad I could hear the tendon twang with every stride. No other day on my running calendar has nearly the importance of Thanksgiving. I'm an endurance runner, and I want to keep going.

The Manchester Road Race is my stage. It provides a big, annual dose of motivation – the most important ingredient for lifetime running.

# 5

# Running and Writing

WORDS HAVE GREAT power. Especially when they are your own words, stories, and affirmations. You can use them to guide, invigorate, and inspire your running.

When Joan Benoit Samuelson was young, she didn't have to think much about why she ran. Benoit dreamed about winning the Boston Marathon, and taking aim at the Olympics. So she hurtled down the road in search of her highest potential, and scored victories at both Boston and the Olympics.

Three decades later, Joan was slower but still hungry for challenges. She needed a new source of inspiration, so she began inventing personal 'stories', her own term, to keep herself on track. This represented quite a change for her – normally a quiet and private individual. She seemed to realise that the stories would elevate her efforts.

In 2008, she decided to chase the 2:50 marathon barrier at age 50. At that year's Olympic Marathon Trials, she finished far behind the young stars, but got a bigger hand than even the winners when she flashed across the finish line in 2:49:08. Mission accomplished.

Two years later, she concocted a different tale for her race at the Chicago Marathon. Twenty-five years after her victory there in 1985, she wanted to run within 25 minutes of her earlier time (2:21:25). Twenty-five years, 25 minutes. Perfect symmetry.

This time Joan missed her goal by a little more than a minute. She finished in 2:47:50. Yet she could hardly be disappointed. Her time established a still-standing marathon world record for fifty-three-year-old women.

Joan obviously has a penchant for creating stories built around the passage of time and her own race times. Several years before turning sixty in mid-2017, she began talking about breaking 3 hours in the marathon in her sixties. No woman runner has ever done this. We'll see how Joan fares.

Other stories don't have to be as competitive as Joan's. I like to keep things simpler and a little more vague. I prefer some wiggle room. So most of my stories start something like this: 'Every run is a new adventure, and every mile is a gift.'

**Keep a training log:** A runner's log or journal is the most basic way to write your story. Even if you only record distances and times, that's a beginning. A log forces you to think about the details of your running, and from those details, many stories and observations will emerge. The great running cardiologist, thinker, and book author George Sheehan, MD, once scanned his journal, and noted: 'I have met my hero, and he is me.'

I know, that sounds a bit egotistic. When I first read this Sheehan sentence forty years ago, I had no use for it. I believed in humility above all else. Now I have softened in this view. We should all attempt an appropriately heroic life, and recognise ourselves for our grit, determination, and successes.

**Collect running quotes:** I don't know any group that enjoys inspirational quotes more than runners. I think this results from the fact that running is both pure and simple, but also demands rigorous hard effort. Great quotes help us rise to the occasion. Keep a collection nearby for ready reference.

Quotes are easy to find in various sources, and I'll let you collect your own. Here's my personal favourite: 'Talk to me not of time and place; I owe I'm happy in the chase.' Shakespeare

**The runner's credo:** The best way to bring together your running stories and life philosophy is to write what I call a 'Runner's Credo'. A Credo captures your essential beliefs and attitudes about a topic. It provides a foundation for all you will encounter – the good and the bad.

Some runners can condense their Credo into a sentence or two. Some need a full paragraph. On the next page, I've provided a longer one that I wrote recently. I'm not suggesting it will work for you. I'm simply offering it as a template. You should edit, condense, and add to it as fits your beliefs and personality. Hint: A little humour goes a long way.

Once you've written your Runner's Credo, put it somewhere in easy reach. On the fridge, or beside your bed, perhaps. You'll want to refer to it often. It will steer your behaviour in a positive direction.

## 6

# The Lifetime Runner's Credo

I AM A RUNNER. I don't run every day, but most days. I rest when I'm injured, when I give birth, when I attend my step-daughter's college graduation, or to attend my father's funeral. A day or two later, I run again. I run because it feels good, and keeps me mentally and physically sharp.

Some days I enter races. I like to challenge myself, and to join the social throng. But I don't define myself by the Olympics, the Boston Marathon, or my 5K PB. I defy all labels: I am runner, jogger, man, woman, young, old.

I am guided by my principles, commitments, persistence, discipline, and resilience. I set the bar high but don't obsess over outcomes. When I am knocked down, I get up.

I run with family and friends because they enhance my life. I run alone for quiet time and to clarify my thoughts. I embrace clean air, clean water, healthy soil, and simple foods. Earth is my home.

After a certain age, I will get slower. No matter. A stopwatch can not measure the quality of my life or the reasons I run. I will adjust and train smart. Running is my play time and my therapy. I run in sun, rain, wind, and snow – through all the seasons of the year, and all the seasons of life.

7

# No More Marathons

I'VE HAD A long career in marathon running. In fact, I'm among the handful of runners who have completed a marathon during each of seven consecutive decades. I ran my first at Boston in 1965 as an eighteen-year-old, and reached my seventh straight decade at Boston in 2017 when I completed the marathon at age seventy.

But there has always been a method to my madness. Through most of my years, I ran Boston only on the fifth-year anniversary of my win in 1968. I respect the marathon distance. Indeed, I fear it. Although I've only dropped out of one marathon, I still can't go to the start line with any confidence that I will finish. The distance is just too great, and the uncertainties too many.

And the recovery? That takes weeks, if not months. Anything less, and I don't think you're putting enough emphasis on proper recovery, and full-body repair.

Those are really important to me. I've got more than 100,000 miles on my body, and am hoping for another 10 or 20 percent. Getting there happy and healthy counts more than racking up a few additional marathon finishes. That's why I plan to stop doing marathons after 2018.

My friends and family don't believe me, but I think it's time to adopt a longer-term perspective. I've paid my dues. There are other horizons in running, and I look forward to exploring them.

Of course I won't stop admiring those who tackle the 26-mile distance. Especially those in my age-group and beyond who continue to roll back the barriers of aging and human performance. When someone shows that one hundred is the new seventy, I'll be the first to stand and cheer.

The number twenty-six will always have special meaning to me. But twenty-five is a nice number, too, a bit rounder. It can be factored down to five days of 5 miles each. I might make that my new marathon.

**Half as long, twice the fun:** I have a friend named Phil, who made an emotional commitment to the marathon in 1995 when he was fifty-two. A veteran of the Vietnam War, Phil wanted to honour his comrades who never came home. Filled with the enthusiasm of a relatively-new runner, he decided to dedicate a marathon a year to his absent friends. Most years, he ran the huge Marine Corps Marathon in Washington, DC.

Phil is a fit, determined guy. He held to his pledge for fourteen years, but then noticed the marathon was beginning to exact a toll. So Phil improvised a new plan. He switched to the half-marathon, and now runs two a year – still 26.2 miles in total – to remember war vets. 'It's something I can manage, and lets me stay true to my personal commitment,' he told me recently.

**Focus on fitness:** Medical and physiology experts are forever trying to determine the minimal exercise goal to achieve optimal health. For some time now, both American and world sports medicine organisations have agreed on 150 minutes a week of modest exercise (like walking) or just half that (75 minutes) of vigorous exercise like running. (Important note: Even very slow running counts as 'vigorous' exercise, according to the medical definition.)

That amounts to as little as 6 to 10 miles a week. Some runners would sneer at this. I'm not one of them, even though I once averaged 100 miles a week for a decade. If 10 miles a week can keep me healthy, I'll gladly use that as my foundation. When I feel like it, I'll run more.

**Listen to your body:** With increasing years, the body talks more. Believe me, mine has become a virtual chatterbox. Once it was stoic. It seemed to barely notice the physical stress I dished out to feet, legs, knees, and more. Now it whines about aches and pains in places I didn't even know existed.

I'm tough enough to ignore most of this whining, but I try not to. Instead I walk and ride my recumbent bike a lot more than I used to. These give me a buzz without a burn. I agree with my longtime friend, marathon expert, and book author Hal Higdon. 'There a point where you have to learn not to do too much,' says Higdon. 'The most important thing is to maintain your quality of life.' That's also the best way to guarantee that you can run again tomorrow.

# 8

# Run-Walk for Life

ABOUT FIFTEEN YEARS ago, I was sharing a meal with South African physician, ultramarathoner, and prolific author Tim Noakes at the annual meeting of the American College of Sports Medicine. Noakes, an MD, had recently finished the most comprehensive running book of all time, *The Lore of Running*. I'm pleased to have an autographed, hard-copy version of the South African original in my personal library. It stretches to 1,277 pages, nearly 100 of which are footnotes.

At this ACSM meeting, Noakes was preparing to deliver a lecture on exercise hyponatraemia – excessive fluid consumption during marathons – and how it could prove dangerous, even fatal to runners. But Noakes is omni-curious, and this particular evening he wanted to show me something else. On his laptop, he found a YouTube video of South African bushmen hunting a springbok.

In the video, a trio of bushmen alternately track and chase a springbok for several broiling midday hours across a South African veldt. They hope to kill it for dinner. Meat contains a far greater calorie payload than their usual tubers.

However, there's no way the bushmen can actually get close enough to use their spears. The springbok has an explosive sprint speed. Every time the men creep almost to spear-range the springbok bounds out of reach.

Until… Until it literally keels over from heatstroke. At that point, the men walk up to the helpless animal, and impale it with their weapons. David Attenborough, the narrator, points out that the bushmen have achieved success through 'persistence hunting'. They refused to give up. They couldn't run fast, but they could walk and jog seemingly forever, even under the relentless African sun.

The springbok's physiology was well suited to a few impressive sprints, but not capable of continuous, endurance exercise. That's an activity humans perform much better. For the bushmen, the pay-off was substantial – tens of thousands of juicy, protein-packed calories.

The bushmen in this video literally walked and ran for their lives – that is, to put food on the table. In an academic paper in 2006, South African Louis Liebenberg reported that he had been observing and taking notes on such hunts for two decades. The longest he had ever witnessed lasted four hours and 57 minutes. Others took from two hours to four hours. Liebenberg concludes: 'Endurance running and persistence hunting may have been crucial factors in the evolution of humans.'

**Follow your biology:** A mix of running and walking appears to be the evolutionary exercise that homo sapiens pursued, and perfected, over several million years. Early humans rarely sprinted – not unless a lion, tiger, or rhino was close on their heels. And they certainly didn't enter marathon races. They didn't attempt to cover 26.2 miles in their best possible time.

But they did move camp slowly with the seasons, the rains, the vegetation, and the vast animal migrations. They did spend hours every day roaming from camp in search of roots, fruits, honey, and other foodstuffs. Occasionally they jogged and walked for several hours to exhaust the weakest antelope in the local herd.

Running and walking is our preferred, evolutionary endurance movement pattern. It also serves at every stage of life – for the eight-year-old and eighty-eight-year-old – and confers extraordinary health benefits to your skeleton, muscles, heart, brain, and more.

**Go easy, go hard:** A run-walk workout mixes the two essential ingredients of aerobic fitness: easy effort and hard effort. The easy walking segment allows you to stay on your feet for anything from 20 minutes to as long as you like. The harder running forces your heart to contract more often and more forcibly, increasing its strength. This gives you the boost in cardiovascular fitness that's directly associated with a longer, healthier life.

**Don't fall into the either/or trap:** I know too many runners who succumbed to faulty either/or thinking. An example: Someone decides to keep running as long as he can maintain an average pace of 10 minutes per mile. When he can no longer hit that target, he quits outright. 'If I can't run at a reasonable pace,' he thinks, 'what's the point?'

Here's what I would say to this person. 'The point is that you can still move, and movement is life. Embrace the changes in your running. Don't give up. Besides, 10 minutes per mile is a completely arbitrary and meaningless number. Don't let it define or limit you. As long as you're moving forward and covering distance, you're still an endurance athlete.

'Don't be a quitter. Be a persist-er.'

# 9

# Total Body Strength

EVERYONE LOSES MUSCLE as they get older. The loss begins when you're in your mid-30s and continues for the rest of life, averaging 3 to 5 percent of total muscle per decade. This has long been one of the most sobering aspects of the aging process. Muscle is what enables us to move, and with less muscle, we will move less. Not a good trend.

When I was in my twenties and early thirties, running more than 100 miles a week, I did nothing but run. I wanted every minute and every hour to deliver the maximum specificity of training. I should have gotten smarter when I dramatically reduced my running at age thirty-five, but I didn't.

It wasn't until retirement age that I mustered the courage and determination to head to a gym awash with strength-building equipment. I had no idea how to use the weights and machines. I simply hadn't paid any attention for the previous forty years.

I set no muscle-head records. But I stuck with my new gym programme and slowly – very slowly – worked out how to do various strength exercises. At first I couldn't help but ask myself, 'How many miles is this worth in my training log?' I soon evolved into guilt-free strength training.

My new routine didn't produce any miraculous results. My weight didn't change, I didn't have to buy larger shirts, and my wife didn't swoon. But after just a few weeks, I actually began to enjoy my trips to the gym, especially the new variety in my weekly workout routine. This was enough to keep me going.

Half a dozen years later, I can report that the first miraculous change has yet to occur. I've got a bit more muscle definition here and there. Still, I'm no bulging Superman – no way, no where, no how. At the same time, I also haven't had an overuse injury since I started my strength programme. And my running, slow though it might be, feels smoother and more coordinated than I remember.

Along with running, I know I'll be strength training forever.

**Hit the weights twice a week:** That's the routine recommended by experts at the American College of Sports Medicine, the most evidence-based fitness group I know. For the most part, I do what they say, and it works out well. I concentrate 80 percent of my strength training on the upper body, in part because that's where I look most like a stringy noodle, in part because I want to retain a good running posture.

I've got a few old buddies who tilt a bit when they run. I'd like to avoid that. Maybe it's just a case of vanity on the roads. Or maybe a strong and balanced upper body can contribute to a piston-like leg swing below. At any rate, I want to continue running tall and straight.

**Practise the plank:** When it comes to strengthening the core muscles, it's hard to beat the basic plank position. Also, there's nothing easier. You simply get down on the floor, lift yourself onto your toes and forearms, and hold that position (with a straight spine) for 20 to 60 seconds. Increase the time as the exercise becomes more comfortable.

Recently, I've begun doing the three-point plank. In this variation, you lift one leg into the air, or pick up one arm. It's an additional challenge, no doubt about it. Another type of plank – the side plank – strengthens the lateral core muscles.

**Build functional strength:** As we age, we tend to have more balance problems. I've certainly noticed this. These arise for a number of reasons, including diminished vision, hearing, and proprioception, plus muscle loss. There are many ways to work on your balance. I often stand on one leg while cooking foods in the microwave.

My favourite routine combines strength and balance. It was recommended to me by Bill Pierce, an outstanding teacher, runner, and author with the FIRST programme at Furman University. Like many modern training experts, Pierce preaches 'functional fitness' – that is, exercises that mimic your primary activity.

For runners, the walking lunge is a top functional exercise. It gets even better when you raise your hands overhead while walking forward. And better again, if you carry modest-weight dumbbells in your hands. This simple movement builds quad strength, core fitness, and balance. You could hardly ask for more.

# 10

# The Power of Positive Thinking

THE MIND IS our greatest asset. Or our biggest enemy. It all depends on how we use it to frame our world. Henry Ford long ago said, 'If you think you can do a thing, or you think you can't, you're right.' Few experienced athletes would disagree with Ford's observation.

Still, it's not enough to simply nod your head in agreement. To get results, you have to actively employ positive thinking. This can prove surprisingly difficult. The mind has a way of conjuring up obstacles on all fronts, from our own inertia to our assumed physical limits.

For many years, I objected to much of the advice proffered by positive talk and visualisation psychologists. I regarded them as overly simplistic, and lumped their ideas into the same category as faith healers and peddlers of magic potions. When I watched them on TV or read their books, I'd scream, 'Show me the results.' I wanted objective, scientific proof – not mumbo jumbo.

I began to change this view when I noticed that many top runners expressed their own variants on positive talk. Two-time US Olympic marathoner Ryan Hall particularly impressed me. Before big events, he would note: 'I'm not sure I'm going to win or run super-fast tomorrow. But I'm open to the possibility.'

The next day, Ryan would run as he had spoken. He attacked the race hard and confident. He didn't always win, but he *did* often excel. He used his positive attitude to open the doors to great achievement.

I also learned about several amazing experiments in which the researchers essentially removed the limits we put on ourselves. They did this by lying to their runner subjects. They told the runners that they were performing a treadmill test at the same speed they had achieved in a prior test.

Only this was a total fabrication. In the second test, the treadmill speed was actually increased by one percent – a substantial difference above an already-all-out effort. Yet the runners were able to complete this second, faster test, because they didn't consider it a big reach. They believed it within their grasp.

Finally, in 2011, the journal *Perspectives in Psychological Science* published a meta-analysis of thirty-two studies on self-talk and athletic success. It confirmed 'the effectiveness of self-talk in sport to facilitate learning and enhance performance'.

**Increase self-control:** 'Yes, I can' works best when it enhances your sense of control. It's less helpful if you set specific but nearly-impossible goals like 'Today I will win my age-group.'

A recent study in *Medicine & Science in Sports & Exercise* followed endurance cyclists who performed a ride to exhaustion before and after two weeks of instruction in positive self-talk. In the second test, the cyclists lasted 18 percent longer, based on four positive phrases they had been practising. The statements were very simple – such as 'Feeling good' and 'You can push through this' – but produced strong benefits.

**Reframe, reframe, reframe:** You might be getting slower, but if you're still in the game, that's a significant victory on its own. A friend named John Cahill was one of the best American age-group marathoners in the late 1990s. At seventy-two, he averaged just over 7 minutes per mile for a full marathon, finishing in 3:05:59.

Twenty years later, Cahill was still running races even though he had slowed to 16 minutes per mile for 5Ks. 'Exercise has kept me happy and healthy, and brought great joy to my life,' he said. 'I don't care how slow I run. I just try to finish before dark. It's way better than sitting in front of a TV with a clicker in my hand.'

**Get real:** I gained a new belief in visualisation techniques when I discovered a psychologist who agreed with my scepticism, but then discovered a better way. Gabriele Oettingen, PhD, has conducted research showing that many positive-visualisation fans spend too much time being positive, and not enough at the hard work of change and achievement. These people fell short in reaching their weight-loss goals.

Oettingen next taught them a technique she calls 'mental contrasting'. They should imagine their success, yes, but also the obstacles they would face, and how they would surmount these hurdles. This approach – positive but real – led to far better weight-loss results. It's also the best way to prepare for your biggest running challenges.

# 11

# Brain Training: Don't stop. Ever. Part II

THE TITLE OF this book is more metaphor than reality. Of course we all stop running at some point. I realise that. I don't want you to think you've been reading advice from a complete nut job. I want you to seriously consider everything I've written.

*Run Forever* can't be a literal reality. It is, however, clear, simple, and bold. That's the way we should all choose to live. Not in the limited world of fatalism. But in the open-ended world of hope, optimism, and personal choice.

Besides, there is lots of *real*-ity in *Run Forever*. From the beginning, I've argued for real actions that real people can embrace to make a real difference in their lives. I've tried to support everything with personal experience, scientific results, and inspiring stories from runners I have known.

I hope you've been impressed with the weight of the evidence. I hope you'll choose to follow the advice and recommendations that ring most true, most useful, and most important to your own life and running.

Ultimately, *Run Forever* is a book about quality of life. Personal fitness offers an arena where we can choose to exert control. Our actions make a difference. Let's just do it.

Running doesn't come with a 'Get out of jail free' card. At times, everyone faces injury, illness, and other obstacles. Still, the setbacks are temporary, while the benefits extend over an entire lifetime. It's lack of exercise – being overly sedentary – that is now recognised as a life- and health-limiting choice.

Perhaps you've seen the cartoon. A physician is talking to his patient, a middle-aged guy who's too large, round, and soft around the middle. The doc has obviously recommended a fitness routine, but the patient says he doesn't have the time.

To which the doc responds: 'What fits your busy schedule better, exercising one hour a day or being dead twenty-four hours?'

**Switch if you must. But don't quit.** In early 2012 I travelled to Houston to meet Dr. Herb Fred. He holds the record for the most verified miles – more than 250,000 – ever run in a lifetime. Dr. Fred, then eighty-two, drove me to his office.

There he showed me his impeccably organised training logs and his trusty treadmill. After being struck by a car while running two decades earlier, Fred had switched to full-time treadmill running. We've kept in touch since 2012, and I watched as his mileage slipped from 3,000 a year to 1,000 a year. Everyone slows down.

In October, 2016, Fred, then eighty-seven, fell off his treadmill. Realising the accident could have been fatal if he had hit his head, Fred knew his running days were over. The next morning, he bought a recumbent bicycle. That very first day, he rode it for nearly three hours. 'Why would I stop exercising now when it has served me so well for so many years?' he told me. 'It has kept me physically and mentally strong.' Dr. Herb Fred represents the spirit of *Run Forever.*

**Start over again:** Like Herb Fred, Mark Covert was an unofficial record holder. He held the American record for the most consecutive days running at least one mile on each and every day. His streak started in 1968, and ended exactly forty-five years later in 2013, for a total of 16,436 consecutive days. Covert was sixty-three.

He stopped because painful injuries had diminished the pleasure he felt while running. The next day, he began riding a bicycle, and has covered 6,000 miles a year ever since. 'It's a joy to be training hard instead of hobbling along,' he said. 'But I wouldn't trade a day of my running for anything.' Again, the *Run Forever* spirit.

**Too soon to stop:** My good friend, teacher, and inspiration Walter Bortz, MD, has spent his life studying how exercise affects the aging process. An ungainly and untalented runner, Bortz nevertheless ran a marathon a year for more than thirty-five years. Even now, in his mid-80s, he continues running and exercising with a teenager's enthusiasm.

He also coined my favourite phrase about exercise and aging. I repeat it more than any other. It goes like this: 'It's never too late to start, and it's always too soon to stop.'

These are words to live by. They are the words I am living by. C'mon along, and join the fun.